Cambridge Elements ☰

Elements in the Philosophy of Martin Heidegger
edited by
Filippo Casati
Lehigh University
Daniel O. Dahlstrom
Boston University

HEIDEGGER
AND KIERKEGAARD

George Pattison
St Andrew's and Copenhagen Universities

CAMBRIDGE
UNIVERSITY PRESS

Shaftesbury Road, Cambridge CB2 8EA, United Kingdom

One Liberty Plaza, 20th Floor, New York, NY 10006, USA

477 Williamstown Road, Port Melbourne, VIC 3207, Australia

314–321, 3rd Floor, Plot 3, Splendor Forum, Jasola District Centre, New Delhi – 110025, India

103 Penang Road, #05–06/07, Visioncrest Commercial, Singapore 238467

Cambridge University Press is part of Cambridge University Press & Assessment, a department of the University of Cambridge.

We share the University's mission to contribute to society through the pursuit of education, learning and research at the highest international levels of excellence.

www.cambridge.org
Information on this title: www.cambridge.org/9781009517379

DOI: 10.1017/9781009417488

© George Pattison 2024

First published 2024

A catalogue record for this publication is available from the British Library.

ISBN 978-1-009-51737-9 Hardback
ISBN 978-1-009-41747-1 Paperback
ISSN 2976-5668 (online)
ISSN 2976-565X (print)

Heidegger and Kierkegaard

Elements in the Philosophy of Martin Heidegger

DOI: 10.1017/9781009417488
First published online: December 2024

George Pattison
St Andrew's and Copenhagen Universities
Author for correspondence: George Pattison, George.pattison@glasgow.ac.uk

Abstract: The work examines the presence and significance of Kierkegaard in Heidegger's work. After setting out the context of Heidegger's reception of the Danish thinker and examining his likely knowledge of his writings, the work first examines key Kierkegaardian concepts that are explicitly present in Being and Time, including existence, 'idle talk' (Gerede), anxiety, the moment of vision, repetition, and the existential significance of death. It is seen that Heidegger regarded Kierkegaard as an essentially religious writer whose work was only indirectly relevant to Heidegger's own project of fundamental ontology. Subsequently, the work considers the place of Kierkegaard in Heidegger's writings from the 1930s onwards, concluding with consideration of the paper Heidegger submitted for the 1963 Paris UNESCO conference marking the 150th anniversary of Kierkegaard's thought.

Keywords: Heidegger, Kierkegaard, existence, anxiety, moment of vision

ISBNs: 9781009517379 (HB), 9781009417471 (PB), 9781009417488 (OC)
ISSNs: 2976-5668 (online), 2976-565X (print)

Contents

Introduction

For close to 100 years, the names "Kierkegaard" and "Heidegger" have often been spoken in the same breath, while judgments as to the nature of their connection have varied widely. At one extreme are those, like the Russian émigré thinker Lev Shestov, who see Heidegger's philosophy as essentially an illegitimate translation of Kierkegaard's biblical thought into the language of Husserlian phenomenology (Guérin, 2011). At the other is the near-total silence of some Heidegger scholars regarding Kierkegaard's significant presence in Heidegger's thought – one recent Companion to Heidegger has only two references to Kierkegaard, and one of these is a quotation from Ernst Cassirer. A comparison of Heidegger's own statements on his relation to the Dane shows a similar ambivalence, as we shall now see.

At the end of 1927, Rudolf Bultmann, a New Testament scholar at the University of Marburg, was approached for advice about a fifteen-line article for the prestigious encyclopaedia *Religion in Geschichte und Gegenwart* (*Religion in History and the Present*). The article was to be about his friend and colleague, Martin Heidegger. Earlier that year, Heidegger had published *Being and Time*, a work that immediately established him as a major presence in German philosophy and that would subsequently come to be regarded as a landmark in European intellectual history. It was almost certainly the recognition of this work's importance that led the editors of the encyclopaedia to seek out an article on the, till then, little published philosopher.

Bultmann and Heidegger had developed a close working relationship since Heidegger's appointment to Marburg in 1923. They shared seminar presentations and met together to study the Gospel of John. Bultmann was eager for the article to do justice to his friend's work and sent a draft of the article to Heidegger for approval. In the draft, Bultmann wrote that "Augustine, Luther, and Kierkegaard were influential for H. in the development of the understanding of Dasein" (Kisiel and Sheehan, 2007: 331).[1] Heidegger amended this passage to read: "Augustine, Luther, and Kierkegaard were philosophically essential in the development of a more radical understanding of Dasein" (Kisiel and Sheehan, 2007: 331). This is clearly a much sharper formulation that places Kierkegaard – along with Augustine and Luther – at the heart of what Heidegger himself regarded as the radical implications of his thought for contemporary philosophy.

---

[1] "Dasein" is a term often left untranslated in Heidegger's commentary, and we shall return to it at a later stage. Very roughly it serves to indicate the existing human being, though leaving open the question as to what this distinctive kind of being "is."

This is striking. No less striking is the reappearance of Kierkegaard in a significantly different triad of thinkers: "Hölderlin–Kierkegaard–Nietzsche," the heading of a section in Heidegger's aphoristic collection *Contributions to Philosophy*, written in 1936–38 but first published posthumously (GA65: 204). Here Heidegger writes of "these three" that it is no accident that, having suffered the "rootlessness" of the modern West in an extreme form, each of them had "to depart early from the brightness of their day," that is, dying young (Kierkegaard) or suffering mental collapse (Hölderlin and Nietzsche). Note that whereas, in 1927, Kierkegaard had been grouped with two epoch-defining figures from Christian history, he now appears together with a thinker and a poet who, for Heidegger, are decisive for the fate of philosophy in the modern world, marking the end of a millennia-long tradition of thought and, in the case of Hölderlin, anticipating a new or second beginning of philosophy.

Kierkegaard's role in this constellation is, however, heavily qualified. In a number of places, Heidegger comments (usually without further explanation) that neither Nietzsche nor Kierkegaard are truly philosophers, but, according to lecture notes from the Winter Semester 1934–5, "men for whom there is no category and whom only a later age will understand" (GA86: 550). Reserving the most decisive role for Hölderlin, Heidegger further distinguishes between Nietzsche and Kierkegaard. In a revision of his earlier opinion, he identifies Nietzsche as the last thinker of Western metaphysics. On this view, Nietzsche's so-called inversion of Platonism exhausts the possibilities for thinking inaugurated by Plato but is unable to move beyond them, resorting to a rather straightforward reversal of values. In this sense, Nietzsche is, after all, of significance, even great significance, for the history of metaphysics. Kierkegaard, however, is not. Indeed, by 1936, Heidegger was saying that "Nietzsche's position vis-à-vis the system [of German Idealism] is fundamentally different from that of Kierkegaard" and that while there may be some justification for linking the two, such linkage was philosophically "untrue and misleading" (GA42: 42–3). A decade later, it has become "fatal and superficial" (GA97: 133). One of the key differences between them is that Kierkegaard's interests were essentially not philosophical at all: "Kierkegaard aims at the *Christian*—original, *New Testament, Protestant* [Christianity] (the opposite of cultural Christianity), and indeed, to the point that he abandons the Hegelian system and works with methods entirely his own" (GA36/37: 279). Indeed, Kierkegaard had nothing to contribute to the history of metaphysics and, despite his opposition to Hegel, remained within the paradigm of Hegelian metaphysics (GA63: 41–2). Through the 1930s and 40s, Kierkegaard is consistently and definitively excluded from the history of philosophy, a "Christian writer" but not a philosopher (GA49: 26). As far as *Being and Time* goes, a note from the war years comments that the question addressed in that work was "completely alien" to Kierkegaard (GA96: 215).

It could seem, then, that in the course of ten years, Heidegger more or less completely abandoned and even denied his own suggestion that Kierkegaard had been "philosophically essential." This may in part have to do with Heidegger's own changing relation to Christianity (remembering that, back in 1927, Augustine and Luther too had been "philosophically essential" to his project) but also his increasing focus on what he would call the "history of being," a history in which a Kierkegaardian focus on the solitary individual might plausibly have little place.[2]

Nevertheless, it will be the argument of this study that for all the apparent changes in Heidegger's evaluation of Kierkegaard, there is an underlying consistency in his attitude and that the later reservations regarding Kierkegaard's philosophical importance are already discernible, albeit differently expressed, in *Being and Time* and even before. This relates to the distinctions Heidegger himself draws between the *existentiell* and the existential and between the ontic and the ontological. I shall explain these distinctions – and their application to the Heidegger/Kierkegaard relationship – more fully later, but, to anticipate, Heidegger sees Kierkegaard as having articulated the passion of Christian faith using the tools provided by what he regards as the ontic science of theology, while his own project is framed in terms of an existential interpretation that is developed in the cause of a fundamental ontology. I shall further argue, however, that these distinctions are not as clear-cut or as stable as Heidegger makes them sound and that his judgment on Kierkegaard therefore raises questions about the nature of his own philosophical investigations.

Our main task, here, however, will be to present a largely chronological dossier of the key moments in Heidegger's engagement with Kierkegaard, with particular emphasis on his own explicit statements about Kierkegaard's role in his thought. In the compass of a short work of this kind, this cannot, of course, exhaust the philosophical issues raised by the Heidegger/Kierkegaard relationship, but it can provide readers with a preliminary orientation that is firmly grounded in the relevant primary sources. *Being and Time* will provide the largest single focus of this dossier, not least on account of Heidegger's progressive self-distancing from his Kierkegaardian "sources" in the following decade. However, to fully see what is going on in *Being and Time*, we have to begin by stepping back and seeing the context in which Heidegger read Kierkegaard,

---

[2] The importance of what she sees as Heidegger's confused relation to Christianity as framing his reception of Kierkegaard is argued especially forcefully in Khawaja 2015.

both the larger context of Kierkegaard's role in German intellectual history and the narrower context of Heidegger's own philosophical development. It will also be necessary to establish a preliminary overview of Kierkegaard's own life and thought so as to have as clear a view as possible as to just what it is that Heidegger is finding interesting here and, indeed, whether or not his reading appropriately reflects Kierkegaard's own concerns. With regard to both Heidegger and Kierkegaard, this short study is necessarily selective and simplifies the work of two of the modern age's most complex and, it might also be said, internally conflicted thinkers. If it serves to assist readers in reading or rereading either or, optimally, both, then it will have done enough.

I shall begin with a brief overview of Kierkegaard's life and thought, proceeding to a survey of his reception in the German-speaking world in the late nineteenth and early twentieth centuries, before moving on to his appearance in Heidegger's thought prior to *Being and Time* and then turning to *Being and Time* itself and to a discussion of the issues that Heidegger's Kierkegaardian references provoke. I shall finally examine some of Heidegger's most important post-*Being and Time* comments on Kierkegaard before concluding with a discussion of the paper he sent for a 1964 UNESCO conference in Paris marking the centenary of Kierkegaard's birth – a paper that curiously contains no mention of Kierkegaard and no citation from his works.

1 Kierkegaard

Kierkegaard, as Heidegger put it, left the brightness of his day early, dying when he was only forty-two. Nevertheless, the fourteen years of his literary activity were remarkably productive across a range of topics and genres. Heidegger is again correct in asserting that central to everything Kierkegaard wrote was the question as to how to live a Christian life that is both faithful to the New Testament and (versus romanticism's medievalist orientation) also appropriate to the circumstances of the modern age. At the same time, Kierkegaard's way of addressing this question involved covering a wide range of topics and employing a variety of styles. Famously, many of his key works were written under a series of pseudonyms and approached the question of how to become a Christian indirectly – by, for instance, presenting non-Christian points of view in such a way as to allow readers to see for themselves what he regarded as their internal contradictions.

I shall here offer a brief overview of Kierkegaard's authorship with particular reference to those aspects that would be of most relevance to Heidegger. I shall pass over the biographical details that have often engaged Kierkegaard commentators and that are easily discoverable elsewhere, except to mention that the defining crisis of his life was to break off his engagement to be married to a young woman, Regine Olsen, and commit himself to a single life, despite the unhappiness that this decision caused both of them and despite his own protestations that he did, nevertheless, truly love her. What is important here is that this decision – what Heidegger would call an *existentiell* decision – both reflected and reinforced Kierkegaard's conviction that becoming a Christian was not just a matter of accepting certain truth-claims but involved a life-commitment that fundamentally affected the whole of one's life in the world.

Kierkegaard had studied theology at the University of Copenhagen, where the atmosphere was a conservative form of romantically inflected Kantian idealism. A charismatic junior lecturer (H. L. Martensen) introduced Hegel into his courses on the history of Christian doctrine and the students, though not the faculty, responded enthusiastically. Kierkegaard himself was unconvinced, not least because he believed that the application of Hegelianism to Christianity would reduce divine transcendence to a form of human consciousness. His Master's thesis (equivalent to a modern doctorate and upgraded to a doctorate in the 1850s) *On The Concept of Irony with Constant Reference to Socrates* can, intriguingly, be read as both pro- and anti-Hegelian. Following his defense of the thesis, he took an extended study-trip to Berlin, where he attended lectures by Schelling and leading Hegelian theologians.

Kierkegaard's breakthrough work was *Either/Or* (1843), published when he was twenty-nine years old and ascribed to the pseudonym Victor Eremita. As the title might suggest, *Either/Or* is in two parts, setting out two contrasting points of view, the aesthetic and the ethical. The first, the aesthetic, is represented by a series of papers of a largely literary character and characterized by intense psychological observation. We soon come to realize that the author's absorption in the aesthetic reflects a basic conviction that the world is essentially meaningless, the product of pure chance, meaning that the best we can do to save ourselves from the boredom of it all is to cultivate more or less sophisticated forms of distraction – art, eroticism, laughter, and even practical jokes. We also learn that an aesthete of this type has lost any meaningful relationship to time, with nothing to value in the past and nothing to hope for in the future. The second part, comprising two long letters addressed to the author of the first, challenges the aesthete to make a genuine life-commitment, such as marriage, to accept the duties that come with that, and to humble himself under the constraints of temporality, living with and finding happiness with the same person, day after day, year after year. This is what Kierkegaard calls the ethical point of view. Those who adopt such a view not only choose a way to live in the external world, they choose themselves – although, as opposed to the autonomous self-production proposed by German idealist philosophers such as Fichte,

Kierkegaard's ethicist declares that we must choose ourselves "from the hand of God" (Kierkegaard, 1987: 217). A short third part consists of a letter from a friend of the ethicist, a pastor on the Jutland heath, arguing that human beings do not have the power to choose such an authentic life and that "over against God we are always in the wrong" (Kierkegaard, 1987: 339–54).

Eight months later, Kierkegaard followed this up with two more pseudonymous books, published on the same day, *Fear and Trembling* and *Repetition*. These take further the question as to whether human beings are in fact capable of justifying their existence through ethical choices. *Fear and Trembling* (which seems not to have greatly interested Heidegger) focuses on Abraham's obedience to God's command to sacrifice his only son, Isaac (although, in the end, God substitutes a ram for the child victim). Christianity presents Abraham as a model of faithful obedience, but Kierkegaard points out that, from an ethical point of view, Abraham is a would-be murderer and has no publicly intelligible justification for what he is doing. *Repetition*, very differently, has the form of a novella, telling the story of a young man who has become engaged to be married but realizes that he cannot follow through and runs away to Stockholm, where he spends his time reflecting on the failure of his love-affair and tormenting himself with the question as to how it is that despite only wanting to act honorably, he has become a bad person, "guilty," in the eyes of the world. As a result, his life has become meaningless and, in his own words, the world "smells" of nothing (Kierkegaard, 1983: 200). He finds comfort in the book of Job, a biblical hero who lost everything but was later restored to his original prosperity by God. Can the young man be restored to his earlier innocence and enthusiasm for life, just as Abraham, who, though he was ready to sacrifice Isaac for God's sake, was happy to receive him back and treasure him as his son and heir? Again, especially, in *Repetition*, the question of time is brought to the fore as the pseudonymous author contrasts the Greek ideal of recollection, as in Plato's theory that all knowledge is founded on the recollection of timeless ideas, with the modern idea of repetition, that is, choosing our life through a relation to the future. By implication, this contrast also embraces Hegelianism, epitomized in Hegel's dictum that the Owl of Minerva, goddess of wisdom, flies at dusk, indicating that it is only when a cycle of history has come to an end that we are able to understand it.

The following year (1844) saw three more pseudonymous works, *Philosophical Fragments*, *Prefaces*, and *The Concept of Anxiety*, published just days apart. *Fragments* again focuses on the question as to whether we are innately equipped with the necessary means of self-fulfillment (what Kierkegaard called the Socratic position) or whether we need a god to save us, concentrating the argument on the Christian claim that it is only through

God's self-incarnation in Christ that we are given the possibility of living as we are meant to live (in Christian parlance, being redeemed). It is here that Kierkegaard develops the idea of paradox, arguing that the unity of the divine and human in the individual person of Christ is unthinkable by reason. He also argues that, from the point of view of the world, there is nothing to distinguish Christ from others, so that his humanity serves as a kind of incognito. It is only by virtue of a leap, a *metabasis eis all genos* (roughly, a shift to another level), that we can have faith in such a possibility. Kierkegaard then goes on to ask how something that happened two thousand years ago can be effective today and how we today are to relate to that historical fact. *Prefaces* is a short work of a largely satirical nature, devoted to mocking several of Kierkegaard's contemporaries. *The Concept of Anxiety*, by way of contrast, addresses the fundamental theological question of sin, its origin and character, and, in particular, the psychological constitution of human beings that makes it possible to speak of us as having fallen from our original possibilities. Because it is specifically mentioned by Heidegger, it is worth looking at this work somewhat more closely.

Kierkegaard starts out by revisiting the biblical narrative of the fall of the first human couple, Adam and Eve. Placed by God in the Garden of Eden, where they have everything they could wish for in order to enjoy a contented life, they are tempted by the serpent (usually understood as a cipher for the devil) to eat the fruit of the tree of the knowledge of good and evil, from which, however, God has forbidden them to eat. Do it, the serpent urges them, because you yourselves will then be like gods. They eat and are expelled from the garden into a world in which they must labor and suffer to survive and reproduce, losing also the gift of eternal life. Dismissing the mythical framework, Kierkegaard sees this as the story of every human individual's passage from the innocence of infancy to adulthood. He described the initial stage of this process as a kind of dream. There is nothing beyond what appears and disappears without effort in this dream-world, but precisely this "nothing," he suggests, engenders anxiety, which, he says, "is freedom's actuality as the possibility of possibility" (Kierkegaard, 1980a: 42) or "the anxious possibility of being able" (Kierkegaard, 1980a: 44). In the moment in which we fully actualize our freedom by choosing to act in a particular way in the world, with some particular aim in view and some particular impact on others, we simultaneously realize one possibility but also lose the many other possibilities that were previously open to us. The prospect of such a choice is compared to vertigo, since what is alarming to the person who stands on the edge of a precipice looking down into the abyss is not that they might fall but that they might throw themselves down. In the grip of this anxiety, Kierkegaard tells us, a person "grasps at finitude," that is, choosing just one way of being in the world (becoming a teacher, a waiter, a spouse) at the cost – or as a way of – suppressing the terrifying multitude of possibilities that freedom continually offers (Kierkegaard, 1980a: 61).[3] Later, Kierkegaard will state that "The possible corresponds exactly to the future. For freedom, the possible is the future, and the future is for time the possible" (Kierkegaard, 1980a: 91). The question of freedom is therefore also the question as to whether we can live with full consciousness of the possibilities that are open to us, or whether (as the ethicist argued) we have to choose just one possibility and allow our values and life-decisions to be determined by that.

The key to Kierkegaard's answer is what he calls "the moment." By this, he does not mean simply the passing moment of time, continually vanishing beneath our feet, but a "moment of vision," the *Øjeblik* (cf. the German *Augenblick*) that literally refers to the glance of the eye, the moment in which we see the world and ourselves for what and who we are. For Kierkegaard, it is such a moment of insight into the temporal constitution of our lives that enables us to live with what would otherwise be the unsettling scenario of unqualified transience. Importantly (not least for Heidegger's reading of Kierkegaard), Kierkegaard conceives this as anticipating the moment in which, as the apostle Paul wrote, our death (i.e., our temporal vanishing) is transformed into eternal life, "in the twinkling of an eye" (1 Cor 15. 52). In the language of Christian theology, it is an eschatological category, from the Greek *eschaton* meaning end, as in God's final judgment of the world at the end of time. As Kierkegaard puts it, "the moment is not properly an atom of time but an atom of eternity" (Kierkegaard, 1980a: 88). Bracketing the mythological elements of this appeal to eschatology, we note, again, that Kierkegaard contrasts this with the Platonic or Greek view of knowledge that he sees as being founded on the recollection of timeless ideas while his own eschatological orientation leads him to identify the task of being authentically human with how we relate to the future.

1845 saw the publication of the enormous *Stages on Life's Way,* one of the relatively few works by Kierkegaard that Heidegger never cited or referred to. *Stages* revisited the themes of *Either/Or* and clarified the threefold "stages" of the aesthetic, the ethical, and the religious. This too involves the story of a failed love-affair and follows the male protagonist's extensive broodings on whether or not he is "guilty." At the start of 1846, Kierkegaard published the last of his first series of pseudonymous works, *Concluding Unscientific Postscript to the Philosophical Fragments*, ascribed to the pseudonymous author of that earlier work, Johannes Climacus – a mere six times as long as the work to which it is

---

[3] The same image is used by Sartre.

a postscript! Again, Climacus-Kierkegaard addresses the question as to how an event so long ago in the past as the life and death of Jesus of Nazareth can be of defining significance for the contemporary world. He rejects the view that it can be made relevant through historical study, as in contemporary attempts to reconstruct the life of Jesus using exclusively historical sources. Nor could it be guaranteed by the ongoing trans-historical testimony of the Church. Instead, everything came to hinge on the individual's subjective passion to find a truth to live by. "Subjectivity is truth," Kierkegaard declares (Kierkegaard, 1992: 118).

This, however, is only the beginning, since the question then is what we mean by subjectivity. Negatively, the attempt to explain this leads Kierkegaard to reject the Hegelian-idealist view that there is a single logic determining the totality of human beings' historical existence and that enables us to explain this in a coherent and systematic way. Kierkegaard is blunt: "A system of existence cannot be given," adding that "in order to think existence, systematic thought must think it as annulled and consequently not as existing" (Kierkegaard, 1992: 118). There are three aspects to this. Firstly, Hegelianism (as portrayed by Kierkegaard) abstracts from the concrete materiality of human life in the world, eating, drinking, blowing our noses, going to the toilet (Kierkegaard, 1992: 306). Instead, it "explains" existence through such categories as "pure being" – but human being is never "pure." We are always – and this is Kierkegaard's second point – "interested" in our lives. Thus, the philosophers' question as to whether the soul is immortal falls short of the existential question: will *I* be immortal? Another way of putting this is that where an objective approach focuses on *what* is the case, subjectivity is interested in the "how" of existence, as in how I experience and am living my life in the world now (Kierkegaard, 1992: 202). But, thirdly (as described in his earlier works), our life in the world is inescapably temporal, so that the issue of subjectivity's "how" also concerns the "how" of our temporality. Where idealist philosophy seeks to relate all phenomena back to an original "being," existing human beings are always in a state of becoming, striving to become or to avoid becoming this or that. As Kierkegaard sums up, "An objective uncertainty, held fast through appropriation with the most passion-ate inwardness, is the truth" (Kierkegaard, 1992: 203). We shall not follow Kierkegaard's argument further at this point, but it is this definition that lays the basis for his subsequent defense of faith as an attitude that certainly doesn't pass the test of objectivity but does correspond to the defining structure of human existence.

At the end of *Concluding Unscientific Postscript*, Kierkegaard owns up to having been the "real" author of the pseudonymous works, although anyone who was interested would probably have known this anyway. It is, in fact, in the person of one of his pseudonyms, Frater Taciturnus, that, in 1846, Kierkegaard was subjected to extended mockery by the satirical journal *The Corsair*, including cartoons that lampooned Kierkegaard himself and made him the butt of malicious sniggering as he walked the streets of Copenhagen. Coincidentally, this raised issues that were engaging him in his next published work, an extended review of a novel entitled *Two Ages* that contrasted the passionate commitment of the generation of the Napoleonic era with the superficiality of the 1840s, epitomized in the opening of Tivoli, one of the modern era's earliest and most enduring theme parks. In the final section of his review, headed "The Present Age," Kierkegaard attacked the social atmosphere generated by an anonymous press that allowed it to attack individuals (such as himself) without fear of any consequences. This was an "age of reflection" in which the readiness for action of the 1790s had been replaced by a culture of "chatter" (*Snak*) in which nothing and nobody had intrinsic value apart from the momentary interest bestowed on it by what we now call the media. It was, Kierkegaard said (writing in his own voice), a culture of leveling, emptying out all substantial values – indeed, it wasn't even a "culture" since it lacked the formative impulse of genuine cultural life (Kierkegaard, 1978: 68–112).

Throughout the period of the first pseudonymous authorship, Kierkegaard had been publishing small collections of what he called "upbuilding" or "edifying" discourses under his own name. Drawing on established traditions of devotional writing, these did not, for the most part, involve explicit doctrinal claims but addressed and nurtured the interior development of individual readers. Subsequent to *Concluding Unscientific Postscript*, he continued to produce such works, although they became more explicitly "Christian." These covered a range of themes, including an important discourse on the theme of death, which, he said, could only be seriously discussed in relation to the earnest thought of one's own death (Kierkegaard, 1993a: 73–76). Another recurrent theme was that of the birds and lilies from the sermon on the mount, representing a call to a simple faith that had shed the compromises and rationalizations of bourgeois religiosity (Kierkegaard, 1993b: 155–212; Kierkegaard, 1997a: 3–91; Kierkegaard, 1997b: 1–45). At the same time, he wrote a short book on *The Point of View for my Work as an Author*, a kind of apologia pro vita sua, explaining that the authorship had been written under the direction of divine providence – even though he had only become aware of this with hindsight. He also clarified the role of the pseudonyms in attempting to bring about an indirect communication of Christianity, by meeting his secular contemporaries on their own ground – the aesthetic – before gradually leading them to see the unsustainability of this position and to prepare them for the radical Christian alternative. One way in which he described this task was, as he put it, to help the individual break free from the crowd, since "the crowd is untruth" (Kierkegaard, 1998b: 105–112).

At the end of the 1840s, Kierkegaard invented a new pseudonym, Anti-Climacus, who spoke for a radical version of Christianity that he himself could not claim to represent. Anti-Climacus was credited with two books, *The Sickness unto Death* and *Practice in Christianity. The Sickness unto Death*, subtitled "A Christian Psychological Exposition for Upbuilding and Awakening," offers an analysis of despair, seen as ubiquitous in the modern world and explained in terms of the self failing to realize the possibilities inherent in its own structure. In a much-cited opening definition, Kierkegaard defines the self as involving a self-relation that, at the same time, is also related to a power, not itself, in which it is grounded. In other words, the self is not something that just "is": we must become ourselves through choosing ourselves and accepting the life-possibilities that have been given to us (Kierkegaard, 1980b: 13–14). Forgiveness, the antidote to despair, is possible and involves much more than forgiveness for moral shortcomings since it means the concrete integration of the self "before God." *Practice in Christianity* develops an account of how contemporary establishment Christianity is very far from realizing what is required for such authentic self-realization and anticipates the all-out attack on the Church that Kierkegaard then delivered in a series of newspaper articles and pamphlets in the last eighteen months of his life, his "Attack on Christendom" (Dan: *Kirkestormen*).

2 Kierkegaard in Germany

2.1 The Translation of Kierkegaard into German

Kierkegaard wrote in Danish and, until the late nineteenth century, was little known outside Scandinavia.[4] However, Danish intellectual life had extensive connections to Germany, and until the Prussian annexation of Schleswig-Holstein, Denmark had a large German-speaking minority. Many Danish scholars were active in Germany, and Kierkegaard himself spent a period studying at the University of Berlin. It was therefore natural that the first "discovery" of Kierkegaard outside Scandinavia was in the German-speaking world. An early and fateful introduction to his thought was the monograph by George Brandes, published in German 1879. Brandes was a Danish literary critic who is also credited with first drawing attention to the work of Friedrich Nietzsche, with whom he also corresponded. On Brandes' view, Kierkegaard's thought was heading in the same direction as Nietzsche's but he remained

---

[4] I am especially indebted in this section to the work of Thonhauser 2016 and Schulz 2009.

limited by his Christian presuppositions. Brandes suggested that, just as Columbus had persisted in believing that the new world he had discovered was the Indies, Kierkegaard too had discovered a new world, the world that Nietzsche would later explore more fully – only he persisted in believing it to be the old world of Christianity.

By the end of the nineteenth century, Kierkegaard was being translated into German on some scale (for comparison, the English translations of his works only got going in the 1930s). Translations had begun in earnest in the 1870s, and from 1909 onwards, a translation of *Collected Works* was underway, completed in 1922, although missing two planned volumes of upbuilding discourses. At the same time, a range of other translations were being made, notably a selection from the journals entitled *Buch des Richters* (Book of the Judge) and a series of selections in the radical cultural journal *Der Brenner* (named after the Brenner pass in the Tyrol). Secondary works were also being translated from Scandinavian languages and the first German studies were appearing, including Theodore Haecker's *Kierkegaard und die Philosophie der Innerlichkeit* (Kierkegaard and the Philosophy of Inwardness) from 1913. Theodore Haecker had translated Kierkegaard for *Der Brenner*, including a number of upbuilding works and, in 1915, the section on "the present age" in which Kierkegaard lambasted the superficial chatter of his time was published by the Brenner press as a free-standing book entitled *Kritik der Gegenwart* (Critique of the Present) and Haecker's commentary made plain that he regarded this as his and his contemporaries' present as well as Kierkegaard's. In 1915 too, *Der Brenner* devoted a special issue to marking the death of the poet Georg Trakl, including some of Trakl's poems and Kierkegaard's discourse "At a Graveside," retitled "On Death." In 1922 Haecker also published a selection of Kierkegaard's upbuilding discourses.

Although interest in Kierkegaard had begun amongst theologians who shared his worries about the fusion of Christianity and modern bourgeois culture, the early twentieth century saw a much wider reception, and the Dane became a recognizable figure in the emerging modernist canon, often linked with Nietzsche and sometimes also with Dostoevsky. Vienna was the main center of this interest and leading figures of intellectual and cultural life, including Rudolf Kassner, Martin Buber, Rainer Maria Rilke, Georg Lukacs, Hugo von Hoffmansthal, Ludwig Wittgenstein and (in Prague) Franz Kafka all testified in varying degrees to his impact. Drawing on accounts from the theologian Paul Tillich, Thomas Mann describes a fictional student club staying up late discussing Kierkegaard on their long pre-First World War rambles through the German countryside (Mann, 1949: 118–19). Heidegger himself speaks of the "arousing years" between 1910 and 1914 in which his generation was gripped by the publication of Nietzsche's *Will to Power*, Kierkegaard, Dostoevsky, Hegel, Schelling, Rilke, Trakl and the writings of Wilhelm Dilthey (Heidegger, 1972: x).

The collapse of Germany and Austria at the end of the First World War intensified the interest in Kierkegaard. Cultural Christianity was discredited through its association with militarism and imperialism, while the Nietzschean project of self-assertion seemed to have foundered in the ignominy of defeat and social collapse. In the introduction to his commentary on Paul's Letter to the Romans, Karl Barth declared that Kierkegaard and Dostoevsky had opened his eyes to the radical nature of Paul's text, especially with regard to the "infinite qualitative difference" (a phrase from Kierkegaard's pseudonym Johannes Climacus) between human beings and God. Barth's commentary has been ranked alongside Spengler's *Decline of the West* and *Being and Time* itself as one of the most influential Germanophone books of the 1920s.[5] By the end of that decade, a substantial secondary literature had grown up around Kierkegaard who had become almost fashionable in German intellectual circles – a kind of "Kierkegaardianism," about which Heidegger would later speak contemptuously (see, e.g., GA28: 311 and GA 29/30: 225).

All of this is important in relation to Heidegger's reading of Kierkegaard and two general points can be noted here.

Firstly, it is clear that Kierkegaard was a familiar name amongst Heidegger's intended readers, and although some of this familiarity could be seen as merely fashionable, many of those who first read *Being and Time* would have at least a broad conception of Kierkegaard's key ideas and cultural significance, with the proviso that the then perception of Kierkegaard was differently focused than that of the early twenty-first century. Kierkegaard scholars in particular have long been somewhat dissatisfied with what they see as Heidegger's failure to acknowledge several important Kierkegaardian themes in his work. In part, this reflects a general feature of Heidegger's approach in *Being and Time*, which does not on the whole engage with specific texts (as opposed to the lecture series that are devoted to key texts from the philosophical tradition), but this doesn't have to be seen in terms of some deliberate policy of concealing his sources. On the contrary, Heidegger could reasonably have presumed that significant Kierkegaardian references would be recognized as such by his readers even without explicit citation.

Secondly, Heidegger was in a position to draw on a wide range of Kierkegaard texts. His knowledge of Kierkegaard has often been connected to the translations appearing in *Der Brenner*, and Heidegger himself refers to how it was through *Der Brenner* that he discovered the poetry of Georg Trakl. However, in an exhaustive study of Heidegger's citations of Kierkegaard, Gerhard Thonhauser has shown that there is no concrete evidence for *Der Brenner* having played an especially significant role in Heidegger's reading of Kierkegaard, although, equally, this cannot be excluded (Thonhauser, 2016: 142–45). Heidegger's actual quotes or allusions point to the *Collected Works* as a main source and suggests extensive familiarity with these (the only volume that he never refers to is *Stages on Life's Way*). Haecker's 1923 selection from Kierkegaard's journals is also referenced, though only twice. Summing up, Thonhauser suggests that despite occasional references to a wide range of works, the main basis for Heidegger's view of Kierkegaard is provided by *The Concept of Anxiety, The Sickness unto Death, Practice in Christianity, The Point of View for my Work as an Author*, and the journals (Thonhauser, 2016: 161), with a brief period when *Concluding Unscientific Postscript* makes a sudden appearance (Thonhauser, 2016: 414–16). However, it should again be emphasized that this doesn't preclude other works from having had some role in the development of Heidegger's Kierkegaard-interpretation. These points will be important when we come to consider Kierkegaard's presence in *Being and Time* more closely.

2.2 The Presence of Kierkegaard in Heidegger's Thought Prior to *Being and Time*

2.2.1 Karl Jaspers' Psychology of Worldviews

We have heard Heidegger mention Kierkegaard as part of the intellectual ferment of the years immediately prior to the First World War, and it seems likely that he read Kierkegaard from that time onwards. However, he does not explicitly engage with Kierkegaard's thought until after the war, when the Dane had become a tangible presence in German intellectual life. In this section, I shall briefly examine three of the key passages where Heidegger explicitly discusses Kierkegaard, namely, his review of Karl Jaspers' 1919 work *The Psychology of Worldviews*, his 1921 lectures on Augustine, and the 1923 lectures on "Ontology: the Hermeneutics of Facticity."

The review of Jaspers' book is both appreciative and critical. On the critical side, Heidegger argues that Jaspers' primary focus on providing a basis for scientific psychology means that he does not sufficiently take into account the underlying question of human beings' concrete relation to the world as such. Jaspers (Heidegger says) sees the human world as encompassed by the infinite stream of life but we can only start making sense of this by focusing on particular aspects, and through that focus, developing a progressive knowledge of the objective world seen from a particular subjective point of view. In this situation, Jaspers gives especial importance to what he calls "limit-situations," such as "struggle, death, chance, and guilt" in which "the most intense consciousness of existence flares up, and this consciousness is consciousness of something absolute."[6] Heidegger notes Jaspers' originality in describing these limit-situations while also mentioning that Jaspers is here also a "student of Kierkegaard and Nietzsche" (GA9: 11/10). This comment introduces a discussion of what will be the much debated term "Dasein." Because the consciousness of existence is at its most intense and even "absolute" in the experience of the limit-situation, i.e., the encounter with what is essentially outside the orbit of the self, our finite Dasein is given to us in the form of a duality or antinomy. That is to say that I, as the being that I am, experience myself as defined by what is not-me, for example, some hereditary guilt by which I feel imprisoned or the death will take my life away. As guilty and mortal I am not, and cannot know myself as, a pure I in the manner of Descartes' pure thinking subject.

Heidegger implicitly affirms much of this but, overall, he thinks that Jaspers' approach already assumes too much. In taking up a theoretical standpoint towards human beings' life in the world, Jaspers overlooks the way in which our engagement in the world is already being shaped in concrete and particular ways prior to our becoming able to step back and take a theoretical or observational (Heidegger even calls it an "aesthetic") attitude towards it. By the time we get round to asking about the nature of things in a theoretical way, our attitude is already "prestructured" in some way or other (GA9: 22/19). In a phrase that has a Kierkegaardian resonance though not explicitly naming Kierkegaard as its source, Heidegger says that this "prestruction" "discloses and holds open a concrete horizon of expectations about which one is anxiously concerned [*bekümmerungshaften Erwartungshorizonts*], and which one develops in each particular context of enacting it" (GA9: 22/19). Another way of putting this that Heidegger goes on to develop is that existence (*Existenz*), that is, human existence, is a "particular 'how' of the self (of the I)" in which "having" my self or being able to say "I am" involves a "basic experience in which I encounter myself as a self" (GA9: 25/29). Noting the echo of Kierkegaard's emphasis on the primacy of the "how" over the "what" in subjective knowledge, we see that the self, Dasein or the "I," is not a single simple entity but is inherently doubled or antinomic: I come to myself as somehow already "there."

---

[6] GA9: 11/10. Heidegger is here quoting Jaspers. "Struggle and chance" suggest Nietzsche, while death and guilt point more towards Kierkegaard. Heidegger will later say that Jaspers' idea of "the absolute" is a secularization of Kierkegaard's religious, Lutheran sense of the word (GA9: 27/23).

This insight further leads Heidegger to the theme of the historical character of human existence. Each of us interprets our world in the light of presuppositions that we have inherited as part of an ongoing collective history of interpretation, which is historically and culturally variable. Jaspers' shortcoming is that he overlooks this and does not recognize that even what we count as "understanding" or "explanation" is the product of a tradition of thinking. The belief that a theoretical account of what a certain being is (for example, what biology tells us about the nature of a particular animal or class of animals) or, for that matter, what goodness "is," is itself shaped by such traditions. But, warns Heidegger, we have to be suspicious of this history and ready to deconstruct it. Again, it is not knowledge that comes first. "The sense of human existence is to be obtained rather from its own basic experience of having itself in an anxiously concerned manner" that is prior to all knowledge and objectification (GA9: 26/30 – "human" is lacking in the German original). What is at issue, then, is the "how" of the self in its pre-theoretical, actual or, as Heidegger puts it, "factical" self-experience.

Although there is much here that resonates with Kierkegaard's thought, he himself is not mentioned for much of this discussion until, in a closing comment, Heidegger makes what I take to be quite a remarkable statement.

> Concerning Kierkegaard, we should point out that such a heightened consciousness of methodological rigor as his has rarely been achieved in philosophy or theology . . . One loses sight of nothing less than the most important aspect of Kierkegaard's thought when one overlooks this consciousness of method, or when one's treatment of it takes it to be of secondary importance (GA9: 36/41).

Heidegger's implication is that this is precisely Jaspers' mistake, but what exactly is the relevant "method" here? Earlier in the review, Heidegger stated that Jaspers' approach "*requires* a more radical type of reflection on method" (GA9: 9/10). Jaspers himself has failed to recognize that his theoretical orientation towards the world is already the product of a certain "immanent method," as Heidegger calls it. This leads to the danger that his conception of the object is not the thing itself, but what Heidegger labels a "surrogate," which, he says, "eventually passes itself off as the genuine phenomenon, whereas the possibility of experiencing the authentic phenomenon vanishes" (GA9: 9/10). Jaspers himself suggests that his method is simply adapted to the requirements of each particular case, but that doesn't answer the objection and still leaves what prestructures experience unexplained. Heidegger doesn't explicitly say so, but it seems, then, that Kierkegaard's "method" is precisely his determination or persistence in focusing on the "how," that is, on the prestructuring of experience by the way in which we live it existentially. It has to be said that this doesn't sound very much like what is normally understood by "method" in science, philosophy, or humanistic study, and more like a certain attitude of mind – and it is certainly not something that lends itself to generating more particular rules or guidelines. It is, however, thought-provoking, suggesting that Heidegger is here aligning himself with Kierkegaard, not only with regard to thematizing such fundamental issues as "the how," "existence," and "Dasein" (which, as we have seen, are intimately interconnected) but also with Kierkegaard's "method" of approaching these issues. There is more to be said here, and we shall return to the implications of what Heidegger sees as Kierkegaard's "method" with specific regard to the "method" of *Being and Time*.

2.2.2 The Kierkegaardian Augustine

Questions of religion were to the fore in Heidegger's immediate postwar lectures. In 1919, he was planning a lecture or lecture series on mysticism but didn't get further than extended notes. In the Winter Semester 1920–21, he gave lectures on the philosophy of religion that were largely focused on St Paul, highlighting the early Christian experience of time, and in summer 1921, he lectured on "Augustine and Neoplatonism." The lectures concentrate on Book X of the *Confessions*, though not (as we might expect) on Augustine's discussion of time and memory but, instead, on his analysis of temptation. As expounded by Heidegger, Augustine depicts the self as constantly having to establish itself through the struggle against the kind of self-loss that Christianity calls temptation and that constantly threatens to draw the emergent self back into the flux of worldly being. A key term is Augustine's *curare*, "care," which, as in English, extends from carefulness, attention, or concern to trouble, sorrow, and anxiety and Heidegger himself would note that this influenced his own idea of care (*Sorge*) in *Being and Time* (SZ, 199 n. iv/492) – although at this stage he uses the German *Bekümmerung*, a translation that will become relevant when we consider the role of Kierkegaard in the formation of this idea.

In the meantime, Kierkegaard is not absent from the lectures on Augustine. The movement of the *Confessions* is determined by Augustine's repeated and passionate quest not only to know God but, as the saint puts it, to know "what I love when I love my God." In relation to this quest, Heidegger's notes read: "1. What really is 'seeking'? 2. What do I really seek? [...] [In] searching for God there is something in me that doesn't just come to 'expression', but something that constitutes my facticity and my concern [*Bekümmerung*] for it [...] What does it mean to say I 'am'? (It turns on winning an 'idea' [*Vorstellung*] of the self, what sort of idea I have of my self. Kierkegaard)" (GA60: 192).

The allusion is not explained, but we have already seen that Heidegger understood the self (Dasein or, at this point, still the "I") as, in Jasper's terminology, fundamentally antinomic and given to itself as a task and a question to resolve, not as some simple stable substance. The introduction of Kierkegaard here, then, suggests that Heidegger sees a fundamental commonality between the Augustinian and Kierkegaardian view of the self-questioning self. This is crucial for understanding the *Confessions*, since, as Heidegger explains, Augustine's search for God also requires him to address the question "How is it as regards my being? (The problem is that 'I am'. I. e., how is it as concerns that, what is it actually? Vita – quaestio [...] Sum=I am – *Existenz* [...])" (GA60: 212). Kierkegaard is not mentioned here but, again, we see the introduction of a key term, *Existenz*, that is central to the cluster of ideas – the self, Dasein, the "I" – that is associated with Kierkegaard, reinforcing the sense that Heidegger's Augustine is being read with Kierkegaardian eyes, preparing the way in which both will feed into the account of the human condition that will be offered in *Being and Time*.

2.2.3 Ontology

In the summer semester of 1923, Heidegger returns to a theme that is already present in his review of Jaspers, namely, how to get behind or pre-empt our own role in forming the world that we experience as immediately given and available for theoretical observation, typically failing to notice our own input into what we thus think of as existing independently of ourselves. As we have seen, Heidegger connects this to the historical character of existence, since we do not start as a tabula rasa but as shaped by our intellectual and cultural inheritance, even though we may experience this as something spontaneous (the child mostly doesn't ask why such and such a character in a fairy-tale is "bad," they simply are "bad"; only later do we see that the witch, for example, may be the victim of a longstanding cultural libel).

A key term in the 1923 discussion is what Heidegger calls "facticity," which, as he now explains, is "our proper Dasein" that is already distorted or limited by the "I." It is, he says, "not of an 'I-like' origin!" (GA63: 29). "One's own Dasein is what it is precisely and solely in its prevailing [*jeweilig*] 'there'" (GA63: 29). But this "prevailing 'there'" is not a timeless essence, as when the human being is described in scholastic philosophy as an individual substance of a rational essence. It is historically determined: it is what it is as it is "today," in its own, contemporary everyday life in the world. This means that our being has to be discovered as it shows itself "In what is [manifest] in the first instance in the present [*Gegenwart*], one [*man*], being with one another, 'our age'" (GA63: 30).

Recognizing this situation, however, exposes us to two risks, both of which Heidegger clearly sees as actually realized amongst his own contemporaries. On the one hand, we might try to understand this "today" in terms of its "most interesting tendencies." For instance, his Marburg colleague Paul Tillich approached what he called "the religious situation" of the present by arguing that it is in the most radical and revolutionary art and literature of the age that its character is most clearly seen.[7] The second error would be to become over-absorbed in the self's own "self-world." Instead of cultural commentary or self-absorption, Heidegger argues that the task of philosophy is to interpret how we are experiencing the everyday world we actually live in with reference to how people speak about themselves and what concerns them.

It is at this point that Heidegger declares that Kierkegaard has provided "strong impulses for the explication being set out here" (GA63: 30[8]) and, precisely with regard to the interpretative or hermeneutic imperative of Heidegger's procedure, we may connect this to his remarks about Kierkegaard's "method" in the Jaspers review. However, in an important early comment that anticipates many of his later remarks, he adds that his own "presuppositions, approach, manner of execution, and goal are fundamentally different." Kierkegaard in fact "makes things too easy for himself" since he is exclusively focused on "his own reflection," perhaps making him guilty of the second error Heidegger has just described (Heidegger wouldn't be the first or last to make this objection). In a second point, Heidegger notes that "He was a theologian and positioned himself within faith, entirely outside philosophy. The present situation is another." When he then immediately goes on to say that what is decisive is to approach our "today" with regard to "something like a character of being" (GA63: 30–1), the implication is that this is what Kierkegaard fails to do.

In a note appended to the lectures, Heidegger offers an extended quote from Kierkegaard, taken from the latter's polemical attack on the established church and typifying his view of what is amiss in the "present age": "To be human today means to be an exemplar of a species endowed with intelligence in such a way that the type is higher than the individual, or that there are only exemplars and no individuals" (GA63: 108). Heidegger's interest in these later polemical writings shows that he is not only drawing on Kierkegaard for the interpretation of the existence of the pre-theoretical Dasein but also shares the Kierkegaard's view that the achievement of this interpretation requires gaining insight into the actual character of the world as it is "today," Kierkegaard's "present age." At the

---

[7] See Tillich 1956 (the English translation of a work that appeared in German in 1926).
[8] See also GA63: 5.

same time, he may also be seeing the Dane as inappropriately over-emphasizing the singularity of the individual and an over-obsession with himself.

3 Kierkegaard's Presence in *Being and Time*

On the basis of the brief survey of Kierkegaard's writings given above, readers with some knowledge of *Being and Time* will see that there is a striking spread of "Kierkegaardian" themes in that work, although the terminology is not in every case the same. The key idea of *Existenz*, the depiction of a world in which language evaporates in "chatter" (Kierkegaard) or "idle talk" (*Gerede*: Heidegger), anxiety, concern, death, temporality, thrownness, guilt, the moment of vision, resolute self-choice, and repetition are key topics addressed by both. Yet Heidegger gives only three footnote references to Kierkegaard and many Kierkegaard scholars have felt that he is guilty of concealing his debt to the Danish thinker. Furthermore, each of these footnotes shows a combination of appreciation and critique, and the overall effect is to downplay any potential influence. Just how important is Kierkegaard to *Being and Time,* then, and in what sense does his presence in that work justify Heidegger's own comment that he had been "philosophically essential" to its genesis?

I have already noted that this apparent neglect is not untypical of Heidegger's relation to his sources. Whereas his lecture series of the interwar years typically involve extended commentary on a range of texts, from Aristotle to Nietzsche (though never Kierkegaard), *Being and Time* offers itself as a phenomenology of the existential condition of Dasein, meaning that its validity does not depend on faithfulness to its textual sources but on its persuasiveness as an interpretation of the beings that we are. There is a great deal of dialogue with a wide range of historical sources going on in *Being and Time*, but Kierkegaard's is not the only case in which this is carried on sotto voce.

A further point to note is that, quite apart from the overall conception and development of *Being and Time*, it includes a considerable number of elements that (versus Shestov) are not anticipated in Kierkegaard. The reflections on language, phenomenology, and the nature of truth that occupy Heidegger's "Introduction" are of a different kind from anything found in Kierkegaard, even if it might be possible to identify some common points. Likewise, there is nothing in Kierkegaard that resembles Heidegger's account of how the world is revealed to us through practical activities such as hammering. Although Kierkegaard, like Heidegger, is much preoccupied with the nature of historical study, the explicit discussion of this in Heidegger is very differently focused. More broadly, Heidegger's interest in developing a fundamental ontological basis for what he calls the ontic sciences is quite alien to Kierkegaard, who had essentially little or no interest in providing a justification for the procedures of academic research.[9]

Nevertheless, some relation to Kierkegaard is clearly present in *Being and Time*, but where – and just what sort of relation is it? One pivotal point concerns the interrelated distinctions between the *existentiell* and the existential and between ontology and ontic science, particularly with regard to Heidegger's reservations vis-à-vis Kierkegaard's significance for philosophy, and we shall return to this in some detail when we have examined Kierkegaard's presence in *Being and Time* more broadly. In a very preliminary way, however, we can say that Heidegger understands what he is doing as involving a deepening of Kierkegaard's account of existence, moving it away from Kierkegaard's focus on passionate subjectivity and towards the guiding question of *Being and Time*: the question of being or, in the technical language of metaphysics, ontology. Before returning to these distinctions in more detail, we shall first examine the three topics where the presence of Kierkegaard is most marked and which are explicitly acknowledged by Heidegger himself: *Existenz*, anxiety and the "moment of vision." I shall therefore begin by focusing on these three points before looking at wider issues regarding Kierkegaard's significance for *Being and Time* and considering Heidegger's own claims regarding this significance.

3.1 Existence/Dasein

Heidegger prefaces his enquiry with the statement that the aim of his enquiry is "to raise the question as to the meaning of being 'anew'," since "we in our time" have no answer to the question as to "what we really mean by the word 'being'" (SZ:1/1). The main text of Heidegger's treatise opens with a programmatic statement in which he declares that it is not his intention to address the question of being in an abstract or merely formal way.[10] On the contrary, he announces, "We are ourselves the entities to be analyzed. The being of any such entity is *in each case mine*" (SZ: 42/67). And, he continues, "The essence of this entity lies in its 'to be'. Its Being-what-it-is (*essentia*) must, so far as we can speak of it at all, be conceived in terms of its Being (*existentia*)" (SZ: 42/67). Most succinctly, he states that "*The essence of Dasein lies in its existence*" (SZ: 42/67).

Later in the text, Heidegger comments in a footnote that "In the nineteenth century, Søren Kierkegaard explicitly seized upon the problem of existence as

---

[9] An exception is the introduction to *The Concept of Anxiety*. See Kierkegaard, 1980a: 9–24. However, this comment does not decide whether Kierkegaard himself didn't develop an ontology, albeit one that was arguably very different from Heidegger's.

[10] Heidegger doesn't mention this, but an obvious contrast would be Hegel's logic, which claims to begin with the pure concept of being before going on to deduce the manifold of our conceptual structure from this simple concept.

an *existentiell* problem, and thought it through in a penetrating fashion" adding that, nevertheless, "the existential problematic was so alien to him that, as regards his ontology, he remained completely dominated by Hegel and by ancient philosophy as Hegel saw it" (SZ: 235, n. vi/494). We shall come back to just what Heidegger means by the distinction between the *existentiell* and the existential, but the main point here is that Heidegger's note establishes a clear connection between Kierkegaard and the defining category of existence/ *Existenz*. Heidegger's footnote is characteristically terse, but in a lecture from 1941, he will explain the relationship between Kierkegaard, the philosophy of existence, and *Being and Time* at greater length.[11] Here he states that the term "*Existenz*" is taken "expressly as the name for the human Dasein and indeed for its being a self (*Selbstsein*), therewith precisely in the sense of the Kierkegaardian restriction [of the term] over against the universally used concept of *existentia*" – a connection, he says, that will be obvious to anyone who knows Kierkegaard's work (GA49: 30). Kierkegaard, then, is present at the very outset of *Being and Time*. We have already seen something of what Heidegger means by "*Existenz*" and "Dasein" in the Jaspers review, where the connection to Kierkegaard was also made and we now need to look at this more closely.

In medieval philosophy, the distinction between essence (*essentia*) and existence (*existentia*) was used to distinguish between *what* an entity is and *that* it is. We can have the idea of something – an oak tree, a mountain range, or an angel – without regard to whether that something actually exists. All oak trees may have died out, the mountain range may be purely legendary, and angels may not exist at all (although the medieval scholastics themselves would not have doubted this). Turning to human beings, then, it would seem that we can distinguish between the essence of a human being and the existence of any actual human being, between the idea of "humanity" and the fact that you and I and all our friends actually exist.

Kierkegaard, we recall, drew attention to what he saw as the fundamental difference between an objective and a subjective approach to any given issue. Objectively, we can engage in a long and interesting discussion as to "what" makes humans human, their rationality perhaps (as in the scholastic definition of "an individual substance of a rational essence"), their tool-making abilities (*homo faber*), or perhaps their capacity for religion (*homo religiosus*) or play (*homo ludens*). As Kierkegaard especially emphasized, we can even discuss whether human beings have an immortal soul. However, this all looks very

---

[11] "The philosophy of existence" is in this context effectively synonymous with the thought of Karl Jaspers, so the heading could read "Kierkegaard, Jaspers, and *Being and Time*."

different when we approach the question subjectively and the general definition of what it is to be human will likely throw little light on the life-decisions I am facing here and now. As regards immortality, the question for Kierkegaard is not whether there is an immortal soul, but whether *I* am immortal or whether, in dying, I cease to be. Consequently, a genuinely subjective thinker is going to be a very different creature from someone who approaches the world objectively. The subjective thinker is focused on the "how" rather than the "what" and admits to an essential interest in his own existence. This existence, moreover, is not over and done with but is still underway, still in a process of becoming, a situation that inserts an essential indeterminacy into the thinker's self-relation – and we remember that, for Kierkegaard, the self is defined fundamentally in terms not of a simple "essence" but as a relation that relates itself to itself and, especially, through the possibilities by which it is related to its own future.

To approach the question of being in terms of *Existenz*, then, is to approach it in terms of how it finds itself being in the world, its "Da" or "there" (Dasein itself is sometimes rendered "being there" as translators attempt to find an English equivalent). To clarify this further, it might be helpful to revisit the term "being" itself. Heidegger's *Sein*, conventionally translated "being," is, like the Latin *esse* and the French *être*, the infinitive form of the verb, "to be." Unfortunately, the English "being" has the form of a present participle, as in "I am being quiet today" or "I am just being." This can encourage a native English speaker to see "being" as a kind of entity that is in a state of being, as indeed when we talk of "a being," for which Heidegger himself uses the German participle *Seiendes* (often translated "beings"). If "to be" is to be applied to some actual thing, event, or state of affairs, then, it has to be conjugated in one or other tense and mood, as in "he is ready," "it was fun," "they will be happy," or "it would have been nice." Just by itself, "to be" is undetermined as regards its manifold possible applications. When Hamlet asks, "To be or not to be?"he is not trying to decide on what is or isn't the case but is considering possible futures. Something of this is conveyed in the Christian existentialist philosopher Gabriel Marcel's idea of the "exigency" of being: our being is not simply *what* we are but what we are required to be or to become (Marcel, 1950: 39–56).[12] We could almost say that it is something like a sense of being called, and it is noteworthy that Heidegger had early on conceived of the idea of being called as the basis for his future revolution in philosophy – only, having abandoned a religious framework by the time of *Being and Time*, "call" can have only a limited, metaphorical sense.[13]

---

[12] Marcel's "exigence" is translated here as "need," which the translator himself notes is scarcely accurate and suggests that the German *Forderung* comes closer to Marcel's meaning.

[13] On "calling" in Heidegger see Pattison, 2019: 13–16, 23–31.

We can, then, only know the meaning of "to be" when we find it made real in some concrete way in the world – when it is "there." But Heidegger is not wanting this to be understood as applying to, let's say, cows in a field. In that case, we have dissolved the tension of the "to be" into the mere factuality of there being cows in a field. In other words, we are still thinking of beings (*Seiendes*) not being (*Sein*). The tension proper to being is only maintained when it is thought from the point of view of that being, Dasein, whose "to be" is still to be determined, still a matter of possibilities and – like Kierkegaardian subjectivity – knowable only from the inside. As Heidegger writes, "Dasein has *in each case mineness*," meaning that "one must always use a personal pronoun when one addresses it: 'I am', 'you are'" (SZ: 42/68). Crucially, Dasein is a "who" (SZ: 45/71), and it is striking that Heidegger's approach to the existential interpretation of this "who" involves the distinction between being who we are authentically and losing our identity in the "they" (SZ: 114–30/149–68), echoing Kierkegaard's distinction between the individual and the crowd. Key to this distinction is that human beings are not just factually there but are to become themselves through the attitude they take to their existence. "Dasein is in each case essentially its own possibility, it can, in its very being, 'choose' itself and win itself; it can also lose itself and never win itself; or only 'seem' to do so" (SZ: 43/68). Again, we hear an echo of the argument of the ethicist from *Either/Or*, that we become ourselves by choosing ourselves – only whereas Kierkegaard further qualified this by adding that we choose ourselves "from the hand of God" (which we could also gloss quite naturally in terms of calling or vocation), Heidegger will go on to locate the exigency of self-choice in what he will call our "thrownness," our just having to deal with how we find ourselves in a world that does not reveal to us any underlying purpose or divine plan.[14]

Again looking back at *Being and Time* from the perspective of the 1941 lecture, Heidegger both acknowledged a kinship with Kierkegaard and Jaspers while distinguishing his own approach from theirs. Conceding that *Being and Time* made extensive use of the term "human Dasein" (which, he says, is merely tautologous and essentially means "human human-being"), he now finds this misleading (GA43: 37). For a start, it encourages the misunderstanding that human being is a kind of being like any other (animal, plant, or divine, as he says). As his discussion proceeds, he will also distinguish between an approach that starts with the human being in order to discover the meaning of being and an approach that is essentially oriented towards the question being but that takes human being as the primary mode of access to that most elusive of questions. The former remains a kind of anthropology and only the latter really addresses

---

[14] On the analogies with Kierkegaardian choice see Han-Pile, 2013: 298–305.

the question of being in a manner appropriate to its subject matter. With an implied Kierkegaardian reference, he now says that the real either/or is either an approach that starts from the human being and remains an anthropology or one that addresses the question of being from being itself (GA43: 72).

Heidegger immediately concedes the difficulty of this last option, which, he says, is compounded by the fact that the history of philosophy has involved a centuries-long distortion and covering over of the question. Consequently, a major element of his later thinking is the attempt to rediscover being by developing a critical alternative "history of being" (for which he typically uses the archaic form of "to be," *Seyn*) and preparing the way for a new or second beginning of philosophy. If what he means by this is often obscure, what is clear is the distance he is now putting between his own way of doing philosophy and that of the overly subjective, humanistic emphases of Kierkegaard and Jaspers. Now it is certainly reasonable to allow that, fifteen years on, Heidegger had become clearer about what he was really aiming at in *Being and Time* itself but it is nevertheless a question – and, for the present writer an open question – as to how far *Being and Time* itself remains within the orbit of the more "humanistic" approach. As we have just seen, Heidegger himself insisted at the outset that Dasein always merits a personal pronoun, a "you" or an "I," and, as he says, is a "who," and in this sense is decidedly "human." If, then, Heidegger's claim is not just that his thought has developed but that it *always was* on an essentially different tack from the philosophy of existence, then this seems more like an unacknowledged retraction or, at the very least, a major readjustment that requires a somewhat fuller justification than Heidegger in fact provides.

3.2 Anxiety

The situation of Dasein ("you" or "I") having to choose its possibilities means that it can fail to choose them in what Heidegger calls an authentic way or, perhaps, it can "seem" to choose them without doing so. This is the typical situation of human beings in what Heidegger calls their "everydayness." Here, instead of each of us authentically choosing our possibilities for ourselves, we live, think, and act according to values and a general understanding of the world that are provided for us by our social milieu. In other words, we live in the same way that everybody lives, as what Heidegger calls "*das Man*," "one," or "the 'they'" (SZ: 126/ 164). This again seems to bring Heidegger into the proximity of Kierkegaard who, as noted above, conducted a vigorous polemic against the leveling of "the present age" and the conformism of the modern bourgeois world in which everyone gets their opinions secondhand. Faced with this kind of conformism, he sought through his writings to detach the individual from the crowd and to confront each individual with responsibility for becoming themselves. Both Kierkegaard and Heidegger also saw this situation as played out in language. For Kierkegaard, the present age has reduced authentic discourse in which people talk seriously and passionately about what really matters to them with "chatter," while for Heidegger the way in which we internalize the opinions and values of the "they" is through discourse (*Rede*) that has become "idle talk" (*Gerede*). Nevertheless, despite the apparent similarities, it is debatable whether or to what extent Heidegger is "taking" this analysis from Kierkegaard. The banality and lack of originality of the average citizen of the modern age have been a recurrent meme of culture critics from the late eighteenth century onwards. Once more, however, we must defer discussion of this until later in order to keep focused on anxiety.

Dasein, then, typically lives an inauthentic life determined for it by the "they." Nevertheless, Dasein cannot stop being Dasein, which means that even in this inauthentic situation, it has the possibility of choosing to be otherwise. There is always a choice – even if we choose to avoid choosing. Awareness of this possibility of choosing can never be entirely repressed but, in the situation of inauthenticity, manifests itself in the form of anxiety. As Heidegger writes, "Anxiety makes manifest in Dasein its *being towards* its ownmost potentiality for being – that is, its *being free for* the freedom of choosing itself and taking hold of itself" (SZ:188/ 232).

Here, Heidegger acknowledges an explicit debt to Kierkegaard, writing in a footnote (that also references Augustine and Luther) that "The man who has gone farthest in analyzing the phenomenon of anxiety – and again in the theological context of a 'psychological' exposition of the problem of original sin – is Søren Kierkegaard" (SZ: 190, n. 4/492). In our brief overview of Kierkegaard's writings, we saw that Kierkegaard did indeed develop the concept of anxiety by means of a commentary on the biblical story of human beings' "fall" from their primordial innocence, a story that Kierkegaard sees being repeated in each individual's life. We also heard how Kierkegaard described anxiety as a kind of vertigo in which, faced with the dizzying prospect of its own multitudinous possibilities, the self "grasps at finitude," i.e., absorbs itself in some finite, limited task or project in which its life is prescribed for it by, e.g., social convention. At the same time, Kierkegaard too saw anxiety as having the potential to help save us from this situation, arousing in us the awareness of another way of being that we could, if we wanted, choose.

In order to understand the full force of Heidegger's footnote, I shall make a brief detour through the larger background of both Kierkegaard's and Heidegger's discussions.

The concept of anxiety is closely related to what Heidegger calls "care" (*Sorge*), a term that, thanks to the German language's facility for compound noun formations, also connects to "concern" (*Besorgen*), meaning our care for the material conditions of our lives, and "solicitude" (*Fürsorge*), meaning our care for one another. Like anxiety, care points us implicitly towards what is future, whether that is towards what we're going to have for lunch or what the neighbor or colleague is expecting from us. Now, both anxiety and care reprise what Heidegger had described as "anxious concern" in the Jaspers review and as "concern" in the Augustine lectures, in both cases using forms of the German *Bekümmerung* to translate Augustine's *cura*, the same word that he now renders as *Sorge*. In a footnote, he notes that the term is not only found in Stoicism but also has a New Testamental provenance, adding that the importance of care had become clear to him in the course of his attempt "to interpret the Augustinian (i.e., Helleno-Christian) anthropology with regard to the foundational principles reached in the ontology of Aristotle" (SZ: 199 n. vii/492). The reference to the New Testament is illuminating since it relates to the term used by Jesus in the Sermon on the Mount, when he says, "take no thought (*mē merimnate*) for the morrow" (in the King James translation) or "do not be anxious about your life" (in the Revised Standard Version), and which, as Heidegger notes, becomes *sollicitudo* (solicitude) in the Latin Vulgate translation.

The Sermon on the Mount, specifically the section that opens with the injunction to "take no thought for the morrow," was a major source of inspiration for Kierkegaard's discourses on the lilies and birds that Christ spoke of as illustrating what a life without such care might be like. One sequence of meditations on this text, from the collection *Christian Discourses*, is entitled *Hedningernes Bekymringer*, that is to say, "the cares of the heathen," which, in a 1922, German translation appears as the now familiar *Bekümmerung* and in English translations as both *The Anxieties of the Heathen* and *The Cares of the Pagans*. The connection to anxiety is made explicit in an expression from later in that collection, where Kierkegaard speaks of "an anxious self-concern" (*ængstelig Selvbekymring*) (Kierkegaard, 1997a: 164). Against the background of the New Testament, then, German, Danish, and English each have a cluster of overlapping and even interchangeable terms that serve to elucidate the kind of anxiety, care, worry, concern, or even just "thought" that Jesus warns against as typifying the life of the pagan world. In Kierkegaard's interpretation of this passage, this is re-applied to those living in bourgeois Christendom, whose "faith" is no more than a routinized church attendance and is more or less identical with the happenstance of being born Danish. This, in short, is the typical mental attitude of citizens of the present age, "caring" or being "concerned about" their material well-being in the world and their social status rather than what Jesus said should be their priority: seeking the Kingdom of God. Later, in *The Sickness unto Death*, Kierkegaard will speak of this attitude even more dramatically as "despair," a persistant refusal to confront the possibility of the radical self-choice that is an irrevocable possibility belonging to our being human.

Returning to Heidegger, I suggest that awareness of this background shows that Heidegger is not basing his view on a few passages of a relatively recent Christian writer but on a widespread and deeply grounded Christian-Stoic understanding of human life in the world that has entered into the common discourse of the West. Kierkegaard is certainly present in this interpretation, but his main role is to have re-envisioned for modern times a model of being human (or, perhaps, failing to be fully and properly human) that is deeply rooted in the New Testament and a tradition of interpretation marked by (but not limited to) such epochal names as Augustine and Luther.

3.3 The Moment of Vision

In a further footnote (that once more links Kierkegaard and Jaspers), Heidegger again acknowledges Kierkegaard's achievement while also indicating a certain reserve vis-à-vis the applicability of Kierkegaard's insights to his own thinking. He writes that

> S. Kierkegaard is probably the one who has seen the existentiell phenomenon of the moment of vision with the most penetration; but this does not signify that he has been correspondingly successful in interpreting it existentially. He clings to the ordinary conception of time and defines the "moment of vision" with the help of "now" and "eternity." When Kierkegaard speaks of "temporality" what he has in mind is man's being-in-time. Time as within-time-ness knows only the "now," it never knows a moment of vision. If, however, such a moment gets experienced in an existentiell manner, then a more primordial temporality has been presupposed, although existentially it has not been made explicit (SZ: 338, n. iii/497).

Again, I shall defer discussion of the important distinction between the *existentiell* and the existential and focus here on just what is meant by the "moment of vision" (Danish *Øjeblik*, German *Augenblick*). Although this has often been glossed in English as "the blink of an eye," the meaning is really the opposite of what happens when we blink. It is not a momentary closing of the eye but a momentary opening, as brought out in the expanded translation "moment of vision." And, as we saw above, it too is a term with a New Testament background, in this case referring to the apostle Paul's "twinkling of an eye" in which we shall be changed from our corruptible mortal lives to our future immortal status (1 Cor. 15.52). In other words, for Kierkegaard, writing within a Christian perspective, it is the moment in which we see ourselves as we truly are, "what we shall be," as another apostle, John, put it (1 Jn. 3.2). It is in this moment, then, that we rise above our anxious concern for our inauthentic lives in the world and see who we are and what we have to be doing with our lives.

This sounds not unlike what many Christian traditions have regarded as a conversion experience, for which Paul himself provides a paradigm case – the one-time Rabbi, fiercely opposed to the new Christian sect to the point of actively persecuting the church until he is suddenly struck down on the Road to Damascus by a vision of Christ calling him to a new life as an apostle. The literature of such conversion experiences is copious.[15] However, while some traditions emphasize the one-off character of conversion ("the hour I first believed"), Kierkegaard is more circumspect. The problem is that such a one-off experience is not true to the ineluctably temporal circumstances of our lives in the world. We may have undergone a radical change, but life goes on, constantly bringing new challenges to which we have to continually respond. In other words, the moment of vision must be repeated again and again – and it is significant that, alongside the moment of vision, "patience" is an important theme of Kierkegaard's religious writings, meaning that we cannot escape the burden of time through a single momentary decision but must repeatedly humble ourselves under the conditions of time. In an example from one of his discourses, he contrasts the courage of a heroic diver, plunging into the water from a great height, with the courage needed to be true to oneself, day after day. The diver's feat is spectacular but it is over in a moment, whereas living with ourselves takes time, the entire time of our lives. "We must crawl before we can walk," Kierkegaard comments, "and it is always dubious when someone wants to fly" (Kierkegaard, 1990: 349). With regard to becoming the self that we are, this cannot be achieved in a single triumphant moment since our very constitution is, as he will say in *Sickness unto Death,* a synthesis of the temporal and the eternal, which is to say that temporality – no less than eternity – belongs to being human as such.

If this is correct, then what are we to make of Heidegger's comment that Kierkegaard's concept is framed by the "now" and "eternity" and that Kierkegaard only thinks of time as a kind of medium "in" which human beings live their lives and does not therefore grasp the interfusion of time and being that Heidegger himself is proposing as an essential step in discovering the meaning of being? Of course, it is not to Heidegger's purpose to enter into the kind of

---

[15] Noreen Khawaja has controversially argued that pietistic conversion provides the model for the anthropology of *Being and Time*. See Khawaja, 2016: 113–15.

exegetical discussion that Kierkegaard scholars live by and, prima facie, his comments are not implausible. Certainly, there are many passages where Kierkegaard speaks in a rather conventionally pious way about turning away from time and towards eternity. On the other hand, we have just noted the importance he attaches to taking time seriously, arguing that the fate of the self cannot be decided in a single "now" but requires the self to humble itself under time and to do so in the mode of patient repetition. As the ethicist of *Either/Or* puts it when arguing against what he calls the mystical abstraction from time for the sake of eternity, "temporality . . . exists for the sake of human beings and is the greatest of all gifts of grace. For the eternal dignity of a human being consist in the ability to acquire a history, and the divine element in human beings lies in their ability to make history coherent, if they wish to" (Kierkegaard, 1987: 250). Seen this way, time is not something external to us but is internal to our constitution as human. Indeed, while the idea of eternity (or, more precisely, of God as the eternal) is integral to Kierkegaard's overall treatment of time, the revelation of possibilities that reveal themselves to us in and through time is the only way we have to find the eternal. As he puts it in *Works of Love*, "By means of possibility, eternity is always sufficiently near to be at hand and yet sufficiently distant to keep a person moving forwards, towards the Eternal, in motion, progressing. Using possibility in this way is how eternity entices and attracts a person onwards, from the cradle to the grave – if only we choose to hope" (Kierkegaard, 1995: 253). In other words, the eternal is not something over against time but something (or, if we are thinking of the theistic God, someone) we can relate to only through the possibilities generated by our lives in time. Although Kierkegaard does speak of the "incommensurability" of eternity and time, God's eternity is not simply the negation of time, as in the scholastic idea of God's timelessness. As Kierkegaard put it in the last sermon, he preached, "He [God] gives time, and He can do that because he has eternity, and he is eternally unchangeable" (Kierkegaard, 1998a: 274). Furthermore, the task of overcoming despair and being the selves that we could be is precisely a task of synthesizing the temporal and the eternal, not turning away from the temporal for the sake of the eternal. In an article that argues for Kierkegaard's concept of time being more radical and more systemically central to his work as a whole, Arne Grøn emphasizes that the outcome of Kierkegaard's writing about time is that "time receives infinite worth" (Grøn, 2023: 553).

It should be said that there is one point at which Heidegger himself gives a more appreciative statement regarding Kierkegaard and the moment of vision. In his lectures on *The Fundamental Concepts of Metaphysics* (Winter Semester, 1929–30), he describes how the basic mood of boredom brings time as a whole to consciousness in a distinctive way, in a moment of vision "in which time itself, as that which makes Dasein possible in its actions, is at work." And, he adds, "What we here designate as 'moment of vision' is what was really comprehended for the first time in philosophy by Kierkegaard – a comprehending with which the possibility of a completely new epoch of philosophy has begun for the first time since antiquity" (GS29/30: 225/150). Although he immediately goes on to deplore the way in which "fashionable" discussions of Kierkegaard fail to notice this, it is striking that – almost uniquely – Heidegger here places Kierkegaard "in" philosophy in a way that has epochal significance for philosophy itself. However, even here, it is possible to understand what Heidegger is saying in terms of his more general view that while Kierkegaard provided unique *existentiell* insights, these nevertheless needed to be worked through with specific regard to the properly existential interpretation of being that he is himself now attempting. We shall therefore now turn to a closer examination of just what this distinction means and its defining importance for understanding Heidegger's relation to Kierkegaard.

3.4 The *Existentiell* and the Existential

Both with regard to the concept of *Existenz* and the moment of vision, we have heard Heidegger speak fulsomely of Kierkegaard's exceptional and penetrating insight. At the same time, he says that this insight is purely *existentiell* and, in the case of *Existenz*, emphasizes that such *existentiell* insight remains "alien" to "the existential problematic." But just what does this mean?

Heidegger himself offers only the briefest of explanations. An *existentiell* approach is one that is defined and decided by Dasein in its own existence. At the same time, this need not involve any further reflection on what he calls "the ontological structure of existence." It is the analysis of this structure that reveals how existence is constituted, what he calls its "existentiality" (SZ: 12/ 33). "Its analytic," he continues, "has the character of an understanding that is not *existentiell* but rather existential" (SZ: 12/ 33) – and it is this structure (or, to be precise, this interlocking network of structures) that *Being and Time* sets out to uncover. It is as part of this task that Heidegger identifies a sequence of existential categories that he calls existentialia, corresponding very roughly to the categories of Aristotelian philosophy, which, however, were developed with a view of theoretical or scientific knowledge and not to the interpretation of Dasein's pre-theoretical way of being in the world (SZ: 44/ 70).

Although Heidegger's formulations are extremely terse, it is not too difficult to see the main point being made. With Kierkegaard in mind, let us take as an example of an *existentiell* choice the decision as to whether or not to renounce a marriage engagement. As Kierkegaard spelled out in many of his published works as well as in his personal journals, such a decision will affect a person's whole life and, in the context of nineteenth century bourgeois life, their social identity. It was to invite being perceived as a scoundrel and would bring shame on the woman spurned. For Kierkegaard, this entailed a scrupulous (and many readers would say over-scrupulous) self-analysis as regards motives and consequences. The whole of his life in the world, inclusive of his moral and religious standing, was in play. Nevertheless, all of this does not of itself necessitate engaging the underlying structures that make a choice of this kind possible. We all have to make major life-decisions, but not everyone's choice will involve the same configuration of personalities and circumstances as Kierkegaard's. If Kierkegaard's question was "Should I marry?," Heidegger's was more like "What makes it possible for me to even consider committing myself to any undertaking for life?"

The point is just as clear if we switch from Kierkegaard to Heidegger and Heidegger's very public and very deliberate choice in Spring 1933 to join the Nazi Party, a choice in which (in his view) the whole future of the German people was at stake. Clearly, in that same year many other Germans, including many of his own former students, made a very different choice. But whichever way they chose and whatever more particular motives and reasons were in play, how could it be possible for a human being to make such a choice in the first place? What is it about human beings that they are able to define who they are in and through such choices? Again, Heidegger's philosophical interest is not in what makes one person a Nazi and another a socialist, but the structures of choice that are in each case presupposed and that reveal something of what it is for human beings to be. It is these, and not the choice of left or right, red or black, that are properly ontological.

In these terms, the difference between the *existentiell* and the existential is closely related to and overlaps with another important distinction, the distinction between the ontic and the ontological. Whereas the category of the *existentiell* applies more to the kind of lived life experiences and decisions of which Kierkegaard's engagement-crisis and Heidegger's political activism serve as examples (though potential examples are as varied as human life itself), the category of the "ontic" is applied to a particular area of being as opposed to the ontological investigation of being as such. The most obvious and most important example of what is at issue here is the relationship between the philosophical questioning of being and what Heidegger calls the ontic sciences, each of which focuses on a particular field of being – Heidegger mentions anthropology, psychology, and biology as examples (SZ: 45/71) but the list extends to the whole range of academic disciplines. In the normal course of events, none of these is obliged to look beyond the limits set by current practice within the field itself. The historian does not have to think about what makes it possible for human beings to pursue the study of history, merely to understand what is methodologically most appropriate to the particular topic being considered. A general theory of the nature of history is probably not necessary in order to produce seminal work on the causes of the French Revolution or the end of the British Raj in India. Coming back to Kierkegaard, we have heard Heidegger speak of him as a "theologian" and working in a "theological context," meaning that although Kierkegaard's penetration in analyzing human beings' *existentiell* situation is exceptional, the tools he uses are those developed by the purely ontic science of theology.[16]

Today, it might seem odd to think of theology as an ontic science on a par with history, biology, or psychology but this was unexceptional in Heidegger's own academic context, and the distinction between theology and philosophy was of particular importance to him in the period up to and including the writing of *Being and Time*. This distinction is most fully set out in the lecture "Phenomenology and Theology," which he gave in 1927 (the year of publication of *Being and Time*). The first published version (in 1970) was dedicated to his Marburg colleague, the New Testament theologian Rudolf Bultmann, with whom he had collaborated extensively in the years up to and including the lecture. Although Heidegger had begun his career in Catholic theology, he was, by the 1920s, closely aligned with Protestant theology, albeit of a non-denominational kind, and, by the end of the decade, had moved to a more clearly atheistic position. The lecture itself reflects an understanding of theology close to that of mainstream Protestant theology and also shows evidence of his reading of the German Reformer, Martin Luther.[17]

Heidegger interprets theology as what he calls a positive science, a term that corresponds closely to what, in *Being and Time*, he calls ontic science and which, in the lecture, he defines as "the founding disclosure of a being that is given and in some way already disclosed" (GA9: 51/43). What does this mean? At its simplest, we may say that human beings have a certain experience of the world around them as composed of inorganic materials, plants, and animals, providing a very preliminary disclosure of being that lays the basis for, respectively, natural science, botany, and zoology. Something similar could be said for each of the familiar sciences, such as anthropology, psychology, and biology

---

[16] Heidegger's distinction is clear, but whether it is entirely persuasive is another matter. Many have argued for there being a "philosophical" element in all the sciences as each is driven to enquire into its own ultimate presuppositions and therefore, even if only implicitly, raise the question as to the kind of being that is being enquired into and, indeed, the kind of being that is doing the enquiring.

[17] On Heidegger's relationship to theology in general see Wolfe 2014, which also gives a fuller treatment of the role of Luther than I am able to offer here.

(mentioned above). But what is the disclosure that lies at the basis of theology? It is, Heidegger suggests, "Christianness" or, more precisely, the lived experience of faith as a way of existence founded on belief in Christ, "the crucified God." As he sums up, "Faith is the believing-understanding mode of existing in the history revealed, i.e., occurring, with the Crucified" (GA9: 54 /45).

Given this definition, theology shows itself to be an essentially historical science, directed to interpreting a mode of existence that can only arise for human beings in an historically specific way, with regard both to the individual's experience of faith and to what makes this event possible, namely, the life and death of a historical individual, believed to be the Christ. It is this focus that subsequently generates the range of standard theological disciplines – the study of the New Testament, church history, the history of dogma, etc. It is also, he says, both systematic and practical. It is systematic in the sense that it seeks to explicate Christian doctrines such as creation, sin, incarnation, redemption, and eschatology in their intrinsic interconnection, and it is practical in the sense that it is directed towards sustaining and enhancing the church's work of preaching and teaching (the view that theology was a practical and not a speculative science, i.e., that it had no essential interest in metaphysical speculation extrinsic to the world of human experience, was particularly associated with Luther's rejection of medieval Christian philosophy). In this sense, theology draws its content from itself and the initiating disclosure of being – faith – on which it is founded.

Now Heidegger willingly acknowledges that faith itself has no need of philosophy but, he argues, theology, the *science* of faith, does. How so? Theology, Heidegger says (and, implicitly, any other positive or ontic science), needs philosophy to demonstrate that its ontic concepts are grounded in an ontology that is "for the most part concealed." But, again, just what does this mean?

Heidegger's example is the relationship between sin and guilt. Sin, he says, belongs to the original disclosure of faith as the basis of Christian existence. This seems straightforward, since Christianity regards faith as freedom from sin and, in a decisive sense, the reversing of original sin (although it could have been relevant, Heidegger doesn't here mention the contextualization of Kierkegaard's concept of anxiety in an interpretation of original sin). But what is it that makes either sin or faith possible?

Heidegger's answer is: guilt. However, we should immediately note that he is emphatically not using guilt in a narrowly moral sense, as when we say someone is guilty of lying, theft, or worse, nor even in a broader sense, as when a person is said to have behaved inconsiderately to their family. Heidegger's term, *Schuld*, has specifically the sense of debt (a meaning reflected in the Scottish version of the Lord's Prayer, which says, "forgive us our debts, as we forgive our debtors" rather than the English "trespasses" or "sins"). A substantial section of *Being and Time* is dedicated to explaining the ontological meaning of guilt, but here there is only space to highlight one essential point: that to see the human being as ontologically guilty is to acknowledge that our being is disclosed to us as fundamentally given or, to put it negatively, that we are not and cannot be the basis of our own being. Although Heidegger does not here spell this out, this corresponds closely to the hugely influential definition of faith given by the theologian F. D. E. Schleiermacher, that it is "the feeling of absolute dependence" (Schleiermacher, 1989: 12–18) as well as to Kierkegaard's definition of the self as needing to become transparent to the power by which it is grounded. However, both Schleiermacher and Kierkegaard are, in a Heideggerian perspective, still drawing their analyses from the *existentiell* experience of faith. Ontological interpretation, however, points us to what is properly basic for human being as such.[18] We can only *be* as dependent on another, whether that other is named "God," "society," or "evolution," meaning that our being as such has the fundamental character of being not self-sufficient but rather "owed." Importantly (not least with regard to the procedure of *Being and Time*), Heidegger further comments that "the name for the procedure of ontology" is "phenomenology," which, he adds, "essentially distinguishes itself from that of all other, positive sciences" (GA9: 67/53).

Heidegger himself calls the role of ontology here a "correction" (*Korrektion*), although he clearly does not mean this is in the sense of correcting a mistake. Theology is not mistaken about sin, and ontology's role is only what Heidegger calls "formally indicative." Theology does not itself need to investigate ontological guilt nor is sin in any way derivative of guilt. In this sense, theology is justified in carrying on as it always has. Nevertheless, the indication of an ontological ground that, in a certain sense, exceeds theology entails what Heidegger calls an "*existentiell opposition*" between theology and philosophy. There cannot be two sciences that account for the whole of human being, a point to which we shall return in the final evaluation of the Heidegger–Kierkegaard relationship. This also means that there can be no such thing as a "Christian philosophy," which, Heidegger says, would be like a square circle (GA9: 66/53)[19] – a clear dig at the tradition of Catholic theology in which he had begun his own philosophical studies.

The distinction between theology and philosophy that Heidegger makes in this lecture helps to explain his approach to Kierkegaard in *Being and Time*. As

---

[18] On the distinction between theological and philosophical views of guilt, see also SZ: 306, n.ii/ 496.
[19] The German expression is, literally, "iron wood."

an *existentiell* writer, the existential analytic of Dasein is "alien" to him; as working from within the presuppositions of Christian theology, he is fated to remain at the level of the ontic and so is not in a position – nor is required to – offer anything like an ontological account of the being that is proper to Dasein. The distinction seems clear enough, but again we note that it is questionable and will require further examination. At the same time, it also throws light on one of Heidegger's footnote remarks about Kierkegaard that has long puzzled commentators. This is where, having praised Kierkegaard's "penetrating" approach to the question of existence, he adds that "there is more to be learned philosophically from his 'edifying' writings than from his theoretical ones – with the exception of his treatise on the concept of anxiety" (SZ 235 n. vi/ 494).

3.5 Heidegger and the Edifying Kierkegaard

Some regard Heidegger's lack of specificity regarding just which edifying writings he is referring to as regrettable and it has certainly leaves scope for questioning just which texts he has in mind. As we have seen, many – though not all – of Kierkegaard's upbuilding and Christian discourses had been translated into German by the time Heidegger was working on *Being and Time* and greater specificity could have been welcome in order to identify just where the center of gravity of Heidegger's reading of Kierkegaard lay. Hans-Georg Gadamer, one of Heidegger's students in the 1920s, recalled Heidegger leading a seminar on Kierkegaard's discourses on the lilies and birds from the Sermon on the Mount.[20] Michael Theunissen identified the discourse "On Death" (to give it its German title) as a likely point of reference for Heidegger's own emphasis on the anticipating of death as the hallmark of authentic existence.[21] Gerhard Thonhauser suggests *The Sickness unto Death* as another possibility.[22] This is intriguing, since this is in fact a pseudonymous work, albeit ascribed to the pseudonym Anti-Climacus (whom Kierkegaard describes as eminently Christian), and it has also been at the center of studies that seek to read Kierkegaard himself as a kind of phenomenologist.[23] Indeed, the opening definition of the self as self-relating and the subsequent unpacking of this in terms of the synthesis of a series of dialectical polarities (finite/infinite, necessity/possibility, temporal/eternal, conscious/unconscious) can seem more like philosophy than edification. However, as Thonhauser notes, the sub-title describes the work as "A Christian psychological exposition for upbuilding and awakening." In other words, even if the form is philosophical, it is to be read

---

[20] See Thonhauser, 2016: 141–42. However, Thonhauser throws doubt on the accuracy of Gadamer's recollection.
[21] Theunissen, 2006.   [22] Thonhauser, 2016: 160–61.
[23] See, e.g., Grøn, 2023: 217–54, 270–85, 304–54; Dahlstrom, 2010: 57–78.

with regard to the help it offers the reader in being religiously "built up" and even "awakened" (one of the buzz words of evangelical Christianity in Kierkegaard's time; Kierkegaard, 1980b: iii).

As we have seen, the self-relating structure of the self that Kierkegaard sets out here and its need to be grounded in a power that is not itself can be closely correlated with Heidegger's view of Dasein as intrinsically twofold, since it is the being that is not simply "there" in the way that rocks, trees, and cows are "there" but is there only by virtue of the exigency of deciding its own concrete way of existing in the world (what Jaspers called its antinomic structure).

However, it is not only in *The Sickness unto Death* that this structure comes to the fore in Kierkegaard. As we have seen in the discussion of care and the connection between anxiety and care, a similar structure can be discerned in various of Kierkegaard's upbuilding writings and, as was also noted, this has a genealogy reaching back through Augustine to the New Testament. In other words, there is no pressing obligation to identify any exact reference here. It seems sufficient to say that Heidegger is putting in play themes to which multiple passages of Kierkegaard's religious writings testify. And, as was also noted, Kierkegaard's own vocabulary varies across his authorship, reflecting a range of usage in Christian tradition itself, especially sharply evidenced in the very varied translations of the relevant New Testament texts.

Writing in the lecture "Phenomenology and Theology," Heidegger approves the description of theology as "systematic," but he insists that its systematic character is not a result of its various findings being fitted into some formal, logically consistent framework but comes from the rigor, radicality, and consistency with which it maintains its focus on the event of faith to which the New Testament bears witness. This is the "founding disclosure" of the domain of being with which theology is to deal and it is thinking in the light of this founding disclosure that makes theology what it is as a science of faith (GA9: 57–8 /47–8). So too with regard to the importance of Kierkegaard for *Being and Time*. It is not a matter of tracking Heidegger's sources to particular passages in Kierkegaard (though the more precise we can be about his exact knowledge of Kierkegaard's texts, the better) but of grasping the issue that Heidegger sees as defining Kierkegaard's overall approach to *Existenz* and that, in his view, provides an eminent approach to clarifying the ontological ground that Kierkegaard presupposes but does not directly thematize.

This can be extended beyond the particular question of the "edifying writings" to the other elements of *Being and Time* that could seem to have received some impulse from Kierkegaard: the analysis of "idle talk" (cf. Kierkegaard's "chatter"), guilt, death, resolute self-choice, repetition, etc. Whether there is a Kierkegaardian "source" behind Heidegger's discussion on any of these or other topics is not really the issue. The point is that if Kierkegaard has indeed thought through the matter of Christian existence in a penetrating manner, as Heidegger says, then he has presented us with a coherent account of existence that grounds and explains each of these. One could even say that, in Heidegger's sense, Kierkegaard was a *systematic* thinker, because all the aspects of his thought are ultimately connected through their shared derivation from the primary focus of his work: the experience of becoming a Christian.

4 Exploring the *Existentiell*

The account of Kierkegaard's presence in *Being and Time* offered in the preceding section has been broadly sympathetic to Heidegger's use of his Kierkegaardian sources and to his account of how the Dane's *existentiell* and ontic (because theological) interpretation of existence relates to his own existential-ontological interpretation. We have also seen that Heidegger's later exclusion of Kierkegaard from the "history of being" that preoccupied him from the 1930s onwards and the judgment that Kierkegaard was not an original metaphysical thinker do not necessarily mark any fundamental change of attitude. The kind of limitations flagged by his categorization of Kierkegaard as an *existentiell* and ontic thinker already define his later reserve. Whatever changes take place in Heidegger's thinking subsequent to *Being and Time* do not therefore involve a change in his basic attitude to Kierkegaard. That Heidegger acknowledged Kierkegaard to be "philosophically essential" to *Being and Time* was not intended to imply that Kierkegaard's thought was simply incorporated into his own interpretative analysis of Dasein. The Kierkegaard who appears in *Being and Time* is, on the contrary, Kierkegaard as – very self-consciously – interpreted by Heidegger.

Nevertheless, we are left with two questions. The first is whether, in every case, Heidegger's understanding of Kierkegaard's *existentiell* thinking is, in fact, faithful to the texts *at the level of the existentiell itself*. The second and perhaps more philosophically important question is whether the basic distinction Heidegger draws between the *existentiell* and the existential and between the ontic and the ontological holds water – and we can ask this question both with regard to Kierkegaard and more generally.

I shall focus next on this second question, namely the question as to the more exact relationship between the *existentiell*/existential and the ontic/ ontological, before concluding this section by considering how well Heidegger in fact reads Kierkegaard in terms of the latter's own *existentiell* interpretation of existence.

4.1 The Existentiell and the Existential (Again)

We recall that, in the Jaspers review, Heidegger especially commended Kierkegaard's method, and although he did not say just what this method was, I suggested that it had to do with Kierkegaard's persistence in focusing on "how" our understanding of the world and of ourselves is prestructured by our existential commitments. In *Being and Time* itself, it is only after three hundred pages that Heidegger turns explicitly to the question of method. " Up till now," he states, "except for some remarks which were occasionally necessary, we have deferred explicit discussions of method. Our first task was to 'go forth' towards the phenomena. But *before* laying bare the meaning of the Being of an entity which has been revealed in its basic phenomenal content, we must stop for a while in the course of our investigation, not for the purpose of 'resting', but so that we may be impelled the more keenly"(SZ: 350/303). Summarizing his argument up to this point, he tells us that this has been directed towards demonstrating "an authentic *existentiell* possibility" (SZ: 312/268), namely, the possibility that Dasein might live its life in the world authentically, since, without this, there is no way of knowing whether or not claims regarding the nature of Dasein's being are anything more than "an arbitrary construction" (SZ: 350/303).

Method, Heidegger now tells us, involves "viewing in advance in an appropriate way the basic constitution of the 'object' to be disclosed" (SZ: 350/303), meaning that the move from the *existentiell* to the existential is not simply a matter of making inferences from the available empirical evidence. Instead, it is taking what has been learned about *existentiell* authenticity as a kind of signpost or directive that existential interpretation follows and which it uses as a basis from which to project an existential structure that provides a larger context or grounding for the existentiell analysis itself. But the right *existentiell* understanding is still essential: "Unless we have an *existentiell* understanding, all analysis of existentiality will remain groundless" (SZ: 360/312), Heidegger writes.

Nevertheless, to the extent that existential ontology involves a projection beyond what is given in the *existentiell* understanding of Existenz, Heidegger cannot avoid the objection that this might be a case of "projection" in a negative sense, i.e., the projection onto the existence of a structure that is essentially alien to it. Indeed, he acknowledges that some will see this existential interpretation as having "the character of doing violence, whether to the claims of the everyday interpretation, or to its complacency and its tranquillized obviousness" (SZ: 359/ 311). But, equally, how are we ever to know whether a particular *existentiell* understanding really is pointing us in the right direction for an ontological interpretation? How can we be sure that the particular *existentiell* scenario that Heidegger (with the help of Kierkegaard and others) set out in the preceding chapters is not something more or less accidentally "pounced upon" (SZ: 361/313)?

Heidegger concedes the charge of circularity and is robust in its defense. "We cannot ever 'avoid' a 'circular' proof in the existential analytic," he reminds us, "because such an analytic does not do any proving at all by the rules of the 'logic of consistency'" (SZ: 363/315). This acknowledged circularity also suggests that when, in the lecture on theology and phenomenology, Heidegger talks about theology qua ontic science presupposing an ontological reference that it does not and cannot itself supply, he is pointing towards what he now speaks of as a "projection."

Recalling that what this is all about is the being proper to the being that has the capacity for being self-relatedly "there," Dasein, what matters is that the resulting account is recognized as convincing by Dasein itself. The answer, in other words, cannot be given except as Dasein's own free affirmation with regard to its own way of being, its recognition that, yes, this is how it *is*. Ultimately, the *existentiell* and the existential are (to borrow a phrase from Christian teaching about the two natures of Christ) inseparably yet unconfusedly joined and Dasein's self-questioning brings us back once more to the domain of the personal pronoun, of mineness, where Dasein must freely take responsibility for the understanding of its own way of being to which its self-questioning has led.

All of this suggests that thinking of the *existentiell* and the existential as two levels, whether of being or understanding, would be misleading. Whereas, in Christian metaphysics, nature and grace (or natural and supernatural) point to two ontologically distinct kinds of being, it is the same being that is at issue in both *existentiell* and existential understanding. Equally, to use a figure associated with Hegel, it cannot be a matter of the *existentiell* being sublated into the existential in the same way that (for Hegelianism) the transcendent God of Judaism and the immanent gods of pagan mythology were sublated into the Christian Trinitarian God who, through the incarnation, is both transcendent and immanent. Rather, the existential is already present, already *there*, in the *existentiell* – if only we look at it in the right way. Being is not like an object situated behind a wall that we have to somehow look over or circumvent in order to get a better view of. The *existentiell* is what it is through its relation to the existential and, equally, the existential is manifest only in and as the *existentiell*. The relationship at issue is open and dynamic, not exclusive; porous, not aporetic. Perhaps, then, we should think less of a circle and more of a self-reflecting spiral as – to use a word Heidegger several times uses in relation to Kierkegaard – we "penetrate" ever deeper and with ever-increasing self-conscious clarity into the mystery of our own being. In these terms, however, there can be no clear dividing line between what is merely *existentiell* and what is properly existential.

A further implication of this is that, at least in some cases, ontology can also become or begin to become an issue within the practice of ontic science. Could this be true of theology? As we have seen, Heidegger regarded theology as the systematic exposition of the event of faith, for which the New Testament is the primary witness. This restriction of theology to the science of faith is strongly attested in the Reformed tradition, whether in Luther's own decidedly anti-philosophical faith or the experience-based theology of F. D. E. Schleiermacher that defined the mainstream of nineteenth- and early twentieth-century Protestant theology in the German-speaking world. It was also an approach that would be championed by Heidegger's colleague Rudolf Bultmann. In this perspective, as we heard, Heidegger regarded a Christian philosophy as equivalent to a square circle. However, this is only one tradition within Christianity and – whether or not we regard it as having succeeded in justifying its claims – the theology of the Western Middle Ages (scholasticism) determinedly sought (like Heidegger himself) to integrate Aristotelian metaphysics into Christian thought and, in doing so, also developed a doctrine of being, according to which being itself (*ipsum esse*) is in fact the truest of the divine names.

For his part, Heidegger regarded this scholastic tradition as having occluded an authentic approach to the question of being. As he explained in a seminar on "The Onto-theo-logical Constitution of Metaphysics" from 1957 (thirty years after *Being and Time*), the God of scholastic metaphysics was a philosophical God combining the categories of first (i.e., God as first cause) and highest (most worthy of worship) and, he argued, before such a God human beings cannot fall on their knees, dance, or pray (GA11: 77/72). At the same time, he acknowledged something like a certain inevitability in the distorting fusion of theology and ontology that had occurred in the Western tradition. Earlier in that same seminar, Heidegger had observed that. "Ontology, however, and theology are "Logies" inasmuch as they provide the ground of beings as such and account for them within the whole" (GA11: 66/59).

But the onto-theo-logical way of thematizing the whole is only one way. A concern for bringing the whole of existence into view is also a driving force in *Being and Time* and, indeed, is pivotal in Heidegger's focus on death as providing a decisive perspective from which to think of human existence as a whole. Existential thinking is not opposed to thinking being as a whole, only to a certain onto-theo-logical way of doing so. But, just like pre-modern Christian metaphysics, the more "existential" theologies of Luther, Schleiermacher, and

Kierkegaard are also oriented towards the whole, and when (for example) they speak of God as creator, this means that what they too are concerned about the whole of being. In the case of a subjective and *existentiell* theology, of course, this is going to work out very differently from either Thomism or biblical fundamentalism. What is at issue is not the validity of pre-modern metaphysics or cosmology but the possibility of human beings coming into a full and adequate relation to who they are according to their defining possibilities. For its practitioners, the *existentiell* passion of faith is a passion that discloses the whole and both reveals and responds to a vision of who we essentially are, in our very being. This is not and cannot be one department of life alongside others in the same way that biology, sociology, and sport science all deal with just one department of life. When, in *Concluding Unscientific Postscript* and elsewhere, Kierkegaard expressly rejects the medieval separation of religion from life, he is also indicating that religion concerns human beings as such and as a whole. Similarly, when *The Concept of Anxiety* takes the myth of Adam's fall as its starting-point, Kierkegaard is clearly assuming that what is to be said will be of concern to all human beings and, in this sense, "Adam" is a cipher for each and every one of us. As Kierkegaard puts it *"every* life is religiously planned" (Kierkegaard, 1980a: 105, translation amended and my emphasis), suggesting that faith is not a more or less arbitrary attitude that is of interest to a self-selecting minority but, on the contrary, offers the optimum outcome to every human life. Obviously, it is another thing entirely to make such claims good in our secular, pluralistic world (and it is definitely not my concern to try to do that here), but it would seem to indicate that Kierkegaard was moving in the direction of some kind of fundamental ontology, that is, a "projection" (to use Heidegger's term) of what human being is as such and what being human requires of us. In this regard, it is telling that three of his discourses on the lilies and the birds about which Jesus spoke in the Sermon on the Mount are built around the topics "to be content with being human," "how glorious it is to be human," and "the blessedness that is promised to being human" (Kierkegaard, 1993b: 155–212). These topics are of a different order from the inspirational manuals that tell us how to succeed, make friends, and be influential – or, for that matter, become better Christians. Whatever we make of Kierkegaard's treatment of them, their implicit claim is to be directing us to the optimum perspective in which to understand human life as such and as a whole.

That being said, it is clearly not the case that every religious text is immediately posing something akin to Heidegger's question of being. Much, perhaps the majority, of religious literature and instruction has a practical and inspirational purpose that directs believers to the concrete tasks of their daily lives rather than inviting them to ponder the meaning of being. In this sense, there might be little to object to in categorizing John Bunyan's *Pilgrim's Progress* (for several centuries the most widely read book outside the Bible in the Protestant world) or François de Sales' *Introduction to the Devout Life* (similarly influential in the Catholic world) as *existentiell* texts that do not push us towards any existential analysis but aim only to address our affective, volitional, and imaginative capacities – working within but not seeking to extend or revise the given ontology of their time. But can the same be said of Kierkegaard?

It is well-known that Kierkegaard was no less energetic than Heidegger in calling for the separation of faith and philosophy. This, he declared, was a bad marriage. Specifically, he spent several hundreds of pages in *Concluding Unscientific Postscript* criticizing the Hegelian attempt to incorporate faith into philosophy, which, he argued, reduced it to a form of human consciousness. Nevertheless (as I have been arguing), Kierkegaard too, not least in works such as *The Concept of Anxiety* and *The Sickness unto Death* or the two works ascribed to Johannes Climacus, writes as if what he is saying concerns human beings as such. In this perspective, Heidegger's own attempt to follow the question of being beyond the exigencies of existence and towards a fundamental ontology might seem to incur the same kinds of criticisms that Kierkegaard made against the Hegelian system, namely, that this is not a philosophy made to human scale, and its fulfillment would point us beyond the realm in which human interests are at home.

The obvious counter to this is that, from a Heideggerian point of view, it is simply restating the either/or that Heidegger himself poses in the previously cited 1941 lectures on Schelling, namely, that there is a basic choice between (1) a philosophy that is primarily interested in the human and that constructs its knowledge of being accordingly and (2) a philosophy oriented towards being that calls on the human as a witness but is ultimately not limited by a human (still less a "humanist") perspective. How we decide this either/or will, I suggest, depend on factors beyond how we read Kierkegaard and Heidegger. Lev Shestov, following Plotinus, argued that the business of philosophy was with *to timiōtaton*, what is most to be feared (or, perhaps better, revered) and it is how we answer this question that will incline us either to follow Kierkegaard's ethico-religious way of upbuilding or to pursue Heidegger's unrelenting questioning of being. But, then again, the ethico-religious might drive us once more towards an ontology while ontology itself might prove to be generative of ethico-religious – or what our age calls "spiritual" – imperatives. From Heidegger's later perspective, this would still mean limiting ontology to a human or even humanist perspective. But a humanist ontology is, nevertheless, still an ontology and, in that light, it seems hard to deny at least the possibility of the Kierkegaardian analysis of existence deepening the *existentiell* into the existential, albeit otherwise than is the case in Heidegger, early or late.

4.2 Kierkegaard's *Existentiell*

In addition to questioning Heidegger's account of the relationship between the *existentiell* and the existential, a further question cannot be avoided. This is the question as to whether Heidegger has in fact appropriately interpreted Kierkegaard's account of existence at the level of the *existentiell*. Of course, if his interpretation at this point is flawed, it also follows that how he understood the relationship between Kierkegaard's writings and his own philosophical work will, at the very least, be skewed. In fact, we have seen that Heidegger's view of Kierkegaard's account of time is, at the very least, open to debate (see Section 2.3), and there are other areas too where his interpretation is questionable. Here, I shall focus on just one: death.

That human existence is properly understood only when we fully acknowledge the inescapability of death, and even, to use Heidegger's vivid expression, "run forward" towards it, was one of the aspects of *Being and Time* that stamped itself on Heidegger's popular image. He himself was aware that the association of his thought with such topics as "anxiety," "nothing," and "death" gave it a certain Kierkegaardian ring, although he regarded this as symptomatic of readers' lack of philosophical discernment (GA49: 31).[24]

Death has, of course, been a major theme of philosophical discourse since the ancient world, and Spinoza's view that the wise think of nothing as little as they do of death is very much a minority report. In an important essay that sets both Kierkegaard's and Heidegger's discussions in the larger context of philosophical and theological history, Michael Theunissen argues for the significance of Kierkegaard's discourse "At a Graveside" for the treatment of death in *Being and Time* – and we recall that this had appeared in German with the title "On Death" in a special issue of *Der Brenner* dedicated to the recently fallen poet Georg Trakl, whose writings Heidegger especially valued (Theunissen, 2006: 328–29).

It is certainly plausible to draw this comparison. At the start of his discourse, Kierkegaard asserts that we can think seriously about death only when we keep our own singular death in mind. In other words, death – more than any other topic – is not something that can be understood with reference to what people

---

[24] Certainly, whatever may be said about the "pessimism" of his focus on death, his account of how the way in which we mostly talk about death actually reveals a strategy of avoidance, even when we ourselves are or someone close to us is terminally ill, remains illuminating and, I would suggest, recommended reading for all involved in care of the dying.

say about it, whether in the manner of everyday chatter, medical science, or even theology. The point is that what is at issue in death is, precisely, *my* death. Death, in this sense, is entirely individuating and, Kierkegaard emphasizes, this is the only way to think about it seriously; everything else is what he calls "sentimental" and this distinction (seriousness/sentimentality) recurs throughout the discourse.[25] This seems at the very least to have some similarity to Heidegger's approach, evidenced in such statements as "Being-towards-death can not evade its ownmost non-relational possibility or cover up this possibility by thus fleeing from it, or give a new explanation for it to accord with the common sense of the 'they'." (SZ: 260/304–5) Or: "Death is Dasein's ownmost possibility. Being towards this possibility discloses to Dasein its ownmost potentiality-for-Being, in which its very Being is the issue" (SZ: 263/307). Both also see death as ultimately inexplicable, in the sense that we cannot come into a right relation to it by way of either poetic imagery or rational explanation. In fully facing up to our own death, therefore, we are no longer thinking about how others might see it or talk about it; we are each doing something that we can only do for ourselves and this brings us in an eminent way into an authentic relation to ourselves.

However, apart from the fact that Kierkegaard understands this situation with reference to human beings' God-relationship while Heidegger focuses on the question of being, there are other, no less significant, differences. Not the least of these is that while Kierkegaard insists that there is a necessary individualization involved in thinking about death, what such thinking reveals is not the solitary individual in their aloneness before the fact of death. On the contrary, it is the essential commonality of the human condition. In this spirit, he sketches two very different responses to the thought that all must die, including those who are unfairly rich and powerful in this world. Seen from a point of view determined by sentiment or feeling, this often takes the form of a sort of gleeful hand-rubbing, relishing the thought that the rich too will get their comeuppance – a kind of Nietzschean *ressentiment*. Seen seriously, however, the fact that all must die reveals our essential equality and, by that token, serves to wean us off from social rivalry (Kierkegaard, 1993: 86–91). What we see here is that, for Kierkegaard, the decisive issue in the confrontation with death is what it means for our relations for others and how we see ourselves in relations to others. But, as Heidegger's reference to death as a "non-relational possibility" indicates, the existential analysis of death takes us in a very different direction, to where the relations with others have no decisive significance. Of course, Heidegger has noted that being-with is a basic mode of Dasein, from which it

---

[25] I am using 'sentimentality' here for the Danish *Stemning*, translated by the Hongs as 'mood'.

follows that how we individually comport ourselves towards death will have an impact on our relations with others. Nevertheless, these relations themselves are not directly at issue in Heidegger's analysis in the way that they are in Kierkegaard. After all, being-with can also be manifest as indifference, hostility, resentment, and much, much more. For Kierkegaard, however, the encounter with death is also an eminent context in which we are to hear and respond to the call to love.[26] The difference has been nicely summarized by David J. Kangas as the difference between Heideggerian being-towards-death and Kierkegaardian "being together with death" (Kangas, 2018: 97–112; see also Pattison, 2013a: 105–26).[27] I take this to be a substantial difference concerning the character of human life in the world and, as such, not reducible to the distinction between the ethico-religious and the ontological thinker.

5 After *Being and Time*

5.1 Heidegger, Kierkegaard, and Nazism

Gerhard Thonhauser has observed that, purely numerically, it is in the period leading up to Heidegger's 1933 entry into the Nazi party and his National Socialist-oriented inaugural speech as Rector of Freiburg University that his references to Kierkegaard are most frequent. Thonhauser acknowledges that he is unable to explain why this is so. However, whatever we make of this curious fact, the actual content of these references does not introduce any significantly new points into his interpretation of Kierkegaard. At the same time, we are obliged to note that the twinning of Kierkegaard and Nietzsche that Heidegger himself started to make in the 1930s had a certain currency amongst National Socialist thinkers.

In October 1933, Emanuel Hirsch, the leading German Kierkegaard scholar of the time and an ardent supporter of the "German Christian" movement that endorsed National Socialist state control over church affairs, published his two-volume *Kierkegaard-Studies* and included a new preface to the translation of the complete works that he had undertaken. This ends with the rally cry: "I hope that the new German time with its fresh daring will facilitate this new translation," suggesting a link between Kierkegaard and the political and social transformation of Germany that was by then underway (Hirsch, 1933: viii).

1934 saw the re-issue of the leading Nazi jurist Carl Schmitt's *Political Theology*, a work that promoted a kind of political decisionism that could

---

[26] See especially the discourse "The Work of Love in Remembering the Dead" in Kierkegaard, 1995.

[27] Charles Guignon notes but does not emphasize this difference, staying with a primary focus on the distinction between the *existentiell* and the existential; see Guignon 2011.

(and I only say "could") be read as a re-application of Kierkegaard's notion of the individual self-affirmation in the sphere of politics. Schmitt includes an extended quote (actually a somewhat doctored quote) from Kierkegaard regarding the priority of the exception over the universal, suggesting, politically, that in a time of crisis, the sovereign power has the right to suspend all laws, including those based on universal principles (Schmitt, 2004: 21; for discussion see Ryan, 2014: 89–134).

Also in 1934, Alfred Bauemler, a leading Nazi philosopher (although Heidegger didn't rate him highly as a philosopher), published an article on Kierkegaard in the *National-Socialist Monthly*, comparing Kierkegaard and Nietzsche and describing them as the only two men of the nineteenth-century who *acted*, that is, who discovered a basis for action in their own responsibility towards themselves rather than allowing their values and goals to be determined for them by society (for discussion, see Pattison, 2013b: 93–95). Of course, neither Nietzsche nor Kierkegaard manned barricades or engaged in imperialist adventures in the way that many of their contemporaries did, but Bauemler's idea of action is specifically focused on the way in which they acted in and through their writing, not circulating ready-made opinions but challenging their readers to break loose of their conformist habits and embrace a whole new view of the world.

If *Being and Time* is read as a kind of voluntarist text, i.e., identifying authenticity with a kind of willful self-choice, Hirsch, Schmitt, and Bauemler might suggest that this is where we are to look for connections to National Socialist readings of Kierkegaard. However, this is also one of the points that Heidegger sees as characterizing the "humanist" misreading of *Being and Time*. At the same time, it has to be said that even if some Nazi philosophers and theologians were enthusiastic about Kierkegaard, it is highly questionable whether Kierkegaard's thought really offers any kind of comfort to a mass movement such as that represented by Nazism. In the Summer Semester of 1933 (shortly after Hitler's assumption of power), Heidegger states that the basic question of philosophy "Still remains, as ever, a matter for our own decision, that we make with regard to our Dasein, that is, for our historical being with others in the membership of the people (*Volk*) " (GA36-7: 14). But this is something that Kierkegaard could not possibly have endorsed. As we have seen, the aim of Kierkegaard's spiritual pedagogy was to wean his readers away from the crowd ("The crowd is untruth") and decide their individual fate through solitary fear and trembling. The trigger for his final attack on the Church was provided in part by the constitutional changes that made Denmark's national church a "people's church" that would remain a national church only as long as a majority of the people (*Folk*) supported it, which is still the situation today. We may add that Kierkegaard spoke also to those, such as Dietrich Bonhoeffer, who, precisely with regard to the priority of the individual Christian conscience over collective values, opposed Hitlerism – in Bonhoeffer's case "even unto death" (on Bonhoeffer and Kierkegaard, see Kirkpatrick, 2011). As to whether the Heidegger of *Being and Time* could have endorsed routing the decision concerning Dasein through the Volk, there remains much room for debate between Heidegger's friends and foes.

5.2 Hegel, Kierkegaard, Nietzsche

After *Being and Time*, Heidegger's later references to Kierkegaard largely repeat or develop points already present there: that Kierkegaard did not offer an existential ontology as such, that he remained within the limits of Hegelian metaphysics, and that he was an essentially religious and, more specifically, Christian thinker. It is in this later period that, on a number of occasions, Kierkegaard is compared with Nietzsche and, at the same time, is quietly excluded from the "history of being (*Seyn*)" that is a major focus of Heidegger's thinking from the 1930s onwards. Quantitatively, Kierkegaard is only minimally present in this period. Nevertheless, the role that Heidegger ascribes to him is not insignificant. Kierkegaard and Nietzsche are the greatest "seers and pathfinders" (*Mahner und Wegbereiter*) for the epochal turning in the history of philosophy that Heidegger sees as gradually taking shape in the twilight of Western metaphysics (GA36-7: 13 [SS33]). In notes for the lecture series in which this comment is found, Kierkegaard seems to be given an even more emphatic role. One note reads "The end and the one who awakens the beginning. The question of Being! How so? Kierkegaard: Christian, 'Existenz' of the individual before God. Time–eternity" (GA36-7: 278).

If Kierkegaard marks both an "end" and a "beginning" in the history of philosophy, the reference to "time–eternity" suggests that the kind of reservations found in *Being and Time* are still in place. As Heidegger says in the lecture itself, "Philosophy is not the concern (*Bekümmerung*) for the solitary existence of the solitary human being as such" (GA36-7:10), although, as he adds, Kierkegaard struck a blow "against the forgetting of human being in German idealism" and "against the dispersal of human being in the rootless multiplicity of its instrumentalism (*Machenschaft*), against its dissolution and splitting off into free-floating domains such as 'culture' and the sciences," a situation that makes the human being little more than an employee, lacking independence (GA36-7: 10). Nevertheless, it remains true of both Kierkegaard and Nietzsche that they were broken by the burden of what they had to say (GA36-7: 11).

Although Heidegger can suggest that, from a certain point of view, Hegel can be seen as the forerunner of Kierkegaard and Nietzsche (GA 36–7: 15), his comments mostly suggest that Kierkegaard has either misinterpreted Hegel or simply missed the point. In some of Heidegger's very final remarks on the Dane (in 1955), he comments that Kierkegaard was mistaken in charging German idealism with absolutizing the human being. Kierkegaard's objections to Hegel are merely "external" since they fail to get the point of what Hegel is doing. The reason is, once more, that Kierkegaard was "an *existentiell* and not a philosophical thinker" (GA86: 781), a point he repeats in two further seminars the following month (GA86: 783, 801). As he had said many years earlier, when Fichte spoke of the productive power of the "I" or ego as generating everything that is "Not-I" this is not hubristic self-absolutizing but a way of drawing attention to the way in which the "I" and the "Not-I" are mutually limiting and therefore actually points to human finitude. The failure to grasp this means that one misses the "innermost driving-force of philosophizing" (GA28: 313). But, as the later remarks show, this is just what Kierkegaard had failed to grasp. In fact, Kierkegaard's understanding of the relationship between being (Heidegger writes the Latin *ens*) and the ego does not even reach the level attained in German Idealism (GA28: 311).

Heidegger, as we have seen, deplores the way in which a misunderstood version of Kierkegaard is used to interpret his own philosophy; nevertheless, when he himself excludes Kierkegaard from philosophy and from the history of being (*Seyn*), this is not to be construed as a simple dismissal. In 1929, he commented that "[Kierkegaard's] true significance is something one cannot talk about and equally cannot write books about, [a fact] which is mostly hidden from his commentators" (GA28: 311). Perhaps we have here a clue as to why Heidegger himself never wrote a book on Kierkegaard or even gave an expository lecture on his work, such as he gave on Plato, Aristotle, Leibniz, Kant, Fichte, Hegel, Schelling, and Nietzsche? More down-to-earth, however, is the obvious explanation that whereas all of these have their part in the history of being, Kierkegaard stands outside philosophy in a way that is even different from that of his fellow "seer and pathfinder," Nietzsche.

5.3 Kierkegaard in the Later Heidegger

Kierkegaard, it is true, scarcely appears in Heidegger's various renditions of the history of being (*Seyn*). Nevertheless, it occasionally seems as if, even here, there are Kierkegaardian echoes. Already in the 1940s, Karl Löwith, a former student of Heidegger, remarked that the "being" that has such a prominent role in Heidegger's "history of being" behaves in a manner very similar to the biblical God: it dwells in mystery and cannot be explained but only evoked; it is the ultimate but inexplicable ground for there being something rather than nothing; it is that which orders and disposes the epochs of history; it is that which we have forgotten but which will reveal itself again in a new, future advent; it is eternal, since it is that which abides as time passes. In view of all this, Löwith asks whether this "being" can do or be all that Heidegger says of it – can it *speak* – without being, in some way, personal: can its self-bestowal on mortals be understood otherwise than an act of gratuitous love? As Löwith wryly comments, "In the end the thinker Heidegger . . . is still today not all that far removed from the religious writer Kierkegaard" (Löwith, 1995: 62).

With Löwith's words in mind, let us briefly note some potentially "Kierkegaardian" moments in the later Heidegger.

It has been several times noted that a major part of Heidegger's later work was marked by the struggle to uncover what had been covered over in the history of Western metaphysics and to prepare the way for a new beginning of philosophy. A key element in this endeavor is that he also identified the culmination of Western metaphysics with the global hegemony of science-based technology. But how might we even begin to break free from this all-encompassing condition of modern life that not only determines manufacturing, transport, and scientific research but war, entertainment, and sport? In the post-war lectures entitled *What is Called Thinking?* Heidegger answers this challenge with the Kierkegaardian-sounding idea of a "leap."

In German as in English commentary, the expression "leap of faith" is routinely associated with Kierkegaard and although he never used this exact phrase it is a fair summary of his idea that neither faith nor, equally importantly, sin occurs as the result of a rationally explicable causal sequence. At a crucial point, there has to be a transition to another kind of thinking and being. This is further associated with his idea of Christ as the paradox, a divine-human person whose character is unique and cannot be grasped by conventional intellectual categories but only affirmed in faith.[28]

This seems a close analogy to Heidegger's view as to how we might break the spell of scientific-technological thinking. In summarizing the third lecture, he invites his auditors to imagine themselves face-to-face with a tree in blossom prior to forming any image or opinion as to what kind of tree it is or how one might describe it. Such moments, he says, make us want to stop for a moment, "as we would catch our breath before and after a leap. For that is what we are now, men who have leapt, out of the familiar realm of science and even . . . out

---

[28] Heidegger several times commented that while Kierkegaard himself saw the paradox as opposed to Hegelian rationality it was, in the terms in which Kierkegaard described it, developed with the tools of that same philosophy that Kierkegaard imagined he was negating.

of the realm of philosophy" (GA8: 44/41). The idea of the step out of science, metaphysics, and a technological view of the world is, indeed, already adumbrated in the pre-war *Contributions to Philosophy*, where a major section is entitled "The Leap" (GA63: 227–89), and it is clearly no passing pedagogical fancy. But this is not Kierkegaard's leap. Where the object of Kierkegaard's leap is faith in Christ as God incarnate (or, equally, the leap from innocence to sin), Heidegger's leap (he tells us) takes us "onto some firm soil. Some? No! But on that soil upon which we live and die, if we are honest with ourselves. A curious, indeed unearthly thing that we must first leap onto the soil on which we really stand. When anything as curious as this leap becomes necessary, something must have happened that gives food for thought" (GA8: 44/41–2). There is a clear difference of intention – and yet the analogy is also striking, not least as the idea of the leap was (as it still is) so widely identified with Kierkegaard. It is also striking, parenthetically, that Kierkegaard too connects the leap beyond reason with detachment from a world increasingly shaped by science and technology. He was consistently attentive to the technological innovations of his day – the steam train, the omnibus, the telegraph, and so on – and, even more importantly, the determination of social ethics and public policy by statistics. His critique of the emergent technological age dovetails with his analysis of the reduction of language to chatter in ways that some find applicable to contemporary critiques of social media. Hubert L. Dreyfus has gone as far as to call him the first critic of the internet (Dreyfus, 2009: 73–89; see also Barnett, 2019 for a fuller discussion of these connections).

Nevertheless, even if it takes us beyond reason, neither Heidegger's nor Kierkegaard's leap comes from nowhere, nor is it context-free. For Kierkegaard, as we have just seen, the leap is a response to Christ's claim to be God incarnate. This claim is not addressed by Heidegger. However, a decisive feature of his later thought is the role of the poet, specifically the poet Hölderlin, who, even more decisively than Nietzsche, pointed the way towards the new beginning that Heidegger sought. But this is not a simple rediscovery of the romantic idea of the poet as the unacknowledged legislator of mankind. As portrayed by Heidegger, the poet comes to almost resemble the Kierkegaardian Christ.

Presupposing the idea of the poet figured in several of Hölderlin's key poems as a kind of sacred orator or bard, whose works are not published in books with a small circulation readership but are spoken at great national gatherings, Heidegger describes Hölderlin (whom he regards as uniquely embodying the essence of poetic vocation) as "establishing the ground on which humans dwell ... preparing the ground for the hearth of the house of history. The poet opens up the chronotope (*Zeitraum*) within which belonging to a hearth and being at home become at all possible" (GA53: 183). This points to the particular significance of Hölderlin's river-poems, celebrating the Rhein and the Danube that define the *Lebensraum* of the German people, as well as the national poem *Germania*. The festive gathering in which the poet speaks his word is, as Heidegger comments in lectures on another poem, *Andenken* (Remembrance), definitive of the time in which the people find their historical destiny. As Heidegger puts it, "*'the feast' is itself the ground and essence of history*" (GA52: 68, Heidegger's italics). In this context, the word that the poet speaks is the word of the people's god, the divinity who calls them into being and summons them to their historical destiny. As such, it is the wedding-feast at which gods and mortals are, through the poetic word, welcomed into fellowship with each other (GA52: 69) and, consequently, the poet whose word inaugurates these festivities stands between human beings and the gods. He is no longer merely human. But he is also not, for that reason, yet a god. As a mediator between gods and humans, he has a role analogous to the theological idea of Christ as mediator. However, Heidegger's poet is admittedly not a God incarnate but a "demi-god" (GA 53: 173). Likewise, the poet is not himself the source of the divine word, as in the Christian idea of Word made flesh but more like a translator: "Thunder and lightning are the language of the gods and the poet is he whose task is to endure and to gather up this language and to bring it into the Dasein of his people" (GA39: 31). But human language is not naturally shaped to be – and in the situation of average everyday *Gerede* certainly no longer is – receptive to the divine word in its original purity. The thunder of biblical and classical epiphanies is experienced by those without insight simply as thunder. Most will only ever hear the poet's word as a hint or sign, calling for interpretation. In Hölderlin's own words, quoted by Heidegger, "We are a sign, uninterpreted/ Without pain are we and have almost/ Lost language in the strange land" (GA53: 202–3). Cast into human language, the divine message is inevitably exposed to misunderstanding. Indeed, to understand it seems to require something like a leap, "The poem . . . is in itself a vortex that snatches us away. Not gradually, but . . . suddenly . . . " (GA39: 45).

Like Kierkegaard's Christ, then, Heidegger's poet bears the holy word of divinity incognito. He is something like a paradox, a speaker of holy things in human form – and here is why it was necessary that Hölderlin (like Nietzsche and Kierkegaard) had to leave the brightness of his day "early" (in his case insanity). His communication of divine things is and, it seems, must be indirect.

The extensive analogies between Heidegger's poet and Kierkegaard's Christ do not, of course, make what Heidegger is saying Kierkegaardian, still less Christian. The fact that he speaks of the poet and not Christ, of gods and not God, of the holy and not faith all indicate that there is an essential difference in play – although, equally, the strong analogies make this a difference that does not preclude a deeper and more thoughtful dialogue between Heideggerian philosophy and Christian faith: more thoughtful, that is, than when the dialogue is restricted to the more or less amicable trading of univocal propositions.[29]

There is one further point at which we see something like a Kierkegaardian echo in the later Heidegger. I have mentioned that one of the key biblical texts to which Kierkegaard returned on many occasions was the section of the Sermon on the Mount in which Christ commended the lilies of the field and the birds of the air as illustrating faith's liberation from the concernful anxiety that attended their lives in the world. It was also noted that where Christ spoke of such concernful anxiety as characteristic of the pagans, Kierkegaard applied this to the citizens of the modern bourgeois world, who, despite being nominally Christian, were preoccupied with materialistic and utilitarian concerns and communicating with one another in essentially non-communicative chatter – people, in other words, not unlike Heidegger's *das Man*, "they."

If liberation from the world defined by chatter and idle talk will require us to leap out of our objectifying, scientific modes of thinking and start learning how to listen for the saving word spoken incognito in the words of Kierkegaard's Christ and Heidegger's poet, it will result in a rather different orientation towards the world and towards our own life in the world. For Kierkegaard, this was the freedom of the lily and the bird; for Heidegger, it is the attitude he calls *Gelassenheit*, "being let go" or "letting-be" (Caputo, 1986: 173–83), sometimes translated "releasement" (Schürmann, 2001: 188–209). The term has also been translated into Latin as *æquanimitas*, equanimity, as in the title of Jacob Boehme's treatise of that title. Heidegger himself takes it from an earlier Christian mystical writer, Meister Eckhart, with whose work he had been familiar at least from the time when he was working on the abortive lectures on mysticism shortly after the end of the First World War. He makes it the subject of an address given in 1955, honoring the composer Conradin Kreutzer, and it also reappears in other writings of the period.[30] The attitude of being set free in such a way as to be open to and accepting of whatever questions, tasks, and possibilities come to us is, as Heidegger was surely well aware, deeply rooted not only in Eckhart but more widely in Christian piety. It would be extravagant to look to Kierkegaard as a "source" for *Gelassenheit*, but it is worth noting that the spirituality of the lilies and birds discourses is closely analogous to what Heidegger articulates in this term and, for both of them, it

---

[29] I have explored the analogies between Heidegger's poet and Kierkegaard's Christ more fully in Pattison 2006.

[30] On the complex interrelationship between the group of texts dealing with *Gelassenheit* see Bernasconi, 2021: 629–31.

indicates a way of being that has been released not only from the concernful anxiety of *das Ma*n but also from subjection to the imperatives of an age of technology.[31] On this point at least, and acknowledging the differences between Kierkegaardian Christology and Heideggerian poetology, Löwith's comment that "In the end the thinker Heidegger . . . is still today not all that far removed from the religious writer Kierkegaard" seems not misplaced.

5.4 Honoring a Kierkegaardian Centenary

In 1963, the hundredth anniversary of Kierkegaard's birth, UNESCO sponsored a conference on his thought in Paris.[32] Papers were presented by, amongst others, Jean-Paul Sartre, Jean Beaufret, Gabriel Marcel, Lucien Goldmann, Karl Jaspers, Jean Wahl, the Danish Kierkegaard scholar Niels Thulstrup, and Martin Heidegger. The roundtable discussion that followed also included Emmanuel Levinas, Jean Hyppolite, Jacques Colette, and another Danish Kierkegaardian, F. Billeskov Jansen. Given the context, it is hard to imagine a more distinguished gathering of minds. Heidegger, however, did not appear in person, and his paper "The End of Philosophy and the Task of Thinking" was translated into French and presented by Jean Beaufret, a major figure in promoting Heidegger's thought in France.

Strikingly, Kierkegaard is not mentioned once in the paper nor, indeed, in the introduction to the English version published in a collection of Heidegger's *Basic Writings* (Heidegger, 1978: 370–72). A contributor to the 1964 roundtable hazards the view that Heidegger's "contribution" is merely a pretext for setting out his own thought (Maheu, 1966: 236). What, then, did Heidegger say in his paper and how, if at all, might it throw light on Heidegger's final reckoning with Kierkegaard?

The paper begins by explaining that ever since 1930 Heidegger has been attempting "to shape the question of *Being and Time* in a more primordial fashion" (GA14: 69/373), which, he suggests requires asking "1. What does it mean that philosophy in the present age has entered its final stage? 2. What task is reserved for thinking at the end of philosophy?" (GA14: 69/373). As Heidegger explains, "end" does not mean mere conclusion, but "the gathering into the most extreme possibilities" (GA14: 70–1/375). In the present age, this is occurring as the practical and theoretical ordering of the world on the basis of science-based technology, which itself is increasingly being "determined and steered" by cybernetics (GA14: 72/376).[33] In this perspective, "The end of

---

[31] The connection is discussed extensively in Kangas 2007.

[32] The conference did not actually take place, however, until April 1964.

[33] Unfortunately, it is not to the point here to examine the prescience displayed by Heidegger in this remark further.

philosophy means the beginning of the world civilization based upon Western European thinking" – which, as Heidegger has made clear, means technocratic thinking (GA14: 73/377). Nevertheless, he asks, might there be some possibility hidden within philosophy that the history that culminates in such technocratic thinking has not thought? If there were, then this would suggest a task for thinking that remains outside the purview of philosophy, metaphysics, and science. Such thinking, he further suggests, "might one day overcome the technological-scientific character as the sole criterion of man's world sojourn" – though only if we ourselves are open to it (GA14: 75/379).

With this question in mind, Heidegger sets out to ask just what "the thing itself," the essential matter of philosophy, really is. For Hegel, he notes, this is the "idea" and, more specifically, the idea thought from the standpoint of the subject. This means that "Only the movement of the idea, the method, is the matter itself. The call to 'the thing itself' requires a philosophical method appropriate to it" (GA14: 77/381). In other words, it is in the practice of philosophizing that the idea comes to show itself for what and as it is: there is no "knowledge" of the thing itself to be had outside of or apart from engaging in philosophical thinking. A hundred years on from Hegel and despite all the differences between them, Husserl too identifies the subjectivity of consciousness as a matter of philosophy. However, neither Hegel nor Husserl reflect on the possibility of anything coming to show itself at all, that is, on the light in which one or other aspect of the world becomes visible. This light, this "brightness" (*Helle*), Heidegger adds, occurs only in a constant interplay or "war" with darkness. The opening of the darkness to visibility is what Heidegger calls "opening" (*Lichtung*), a word he traces back to the word for a forest clearing in which light is able to break into the dense thickness of the forest itself. What is basic here, however, is not the light but the clearing that allows the light to pour in and "play" with darkness.

This opening, Heidegger says (borrowing a term from Goethe) is a "primal phenomenon" (GA14: 81/385). As such, it will never become the object of some possible intuition and is prior to all subjectivity. Poetically, it is described by Parmenides as "the untrembling heart of all unconcealment," evoking Heidegger's defining idea of truth as unconcealment (*alētheia*), as opposed to the "correct" correspondence of thought and object (GA14: 81/387). But it is just this unconcealment – in which (Heidegger says) "being and thinking and their belonging together exist" (GA14: 85/388) – that philosophy as metaphysics has forgotten. This is not, however, a simple error on the part of philosophy, since, Heidegger says, what *alētheia* is remains concealed and this concealment is not some mere accident but the result of a "self-concealment, concealment, *lēthē*" at the "heart of *alētheia*" (GA14: 88/390).

Heidegger is well aware that many will dismiss this as "unfounded mysticism," "bad mythology," and "ruinous irrationalism" (GA14: 88/391). Nevertheless, it allows for a kind of thinking that is "more sober-minded than the incessant frenzy of rationalization and the intoxicating quality of cybernetics" (GA14: 89/391). For such thinking, the theme "being and time" becomes instead "opening and presence" or, as Heidegger further asks, "But where does the opening come from and how is it given? What speaks in the 'There is / It gives?'" (GA14: 90/392).[34]

In many ways, Heidegger's paper serves as an effective and very concise summary of themes dominating his thinking of the post-war period, but was "Kierkegaard" just a pretext for him to set out his own thought?[35] Responding to this charge, Jean Beaufret offers a couple of suggestions, though he emphasizes that these are only suggestions, no more. The first is that just as Kierkegaard found himself having to reinvent Christianity in view of the degeneration of original Christianity into the social conformism of modern "Christendom," so too Heidegger found himself having to reinvent or find a new way of doing philosophy in face of the evolution of Western metaphysics into the ideology of technocratic and cybernetic thinking (Maheu, 1966: 256–57). The second is that, with regard to the subjectivization of philosophy in Hegel and Husserl, Kierkegaard offered an alternative way of thinking subjectivity to which his self-description as a "poet of the religious" offers a clue. This would identify Kierkegaard as offering a way of thinking that is outside the opposition rational–irrational, i.e., a way of thinking resonant with what, in the paper, Heidegger calls the task of thinking outside of or beyond the limits of rational metaphysics. Drawing a parallel between the relationships Descartes/Pascal and Hegel/Kierkegaard, Beaufret says that in this way and "measured by the standard of his time, [Kierkegaard] becomes the philosopher's anti-philosopher, born of the same subjectivity" (Maheu, 1966: 258–59).

Both of these proposals have merit. Certainly, as we have seen, though all too briefly, Kierkegaard, like Heidegger, saw his task as a critical response not only to the abstract logic of Hegelianism but also to the technologized mass-society that Hegelian abstraction, qua abstraction from the concrete and individual, represented at a theoretical level. Likewise, as I shall consider further in the next section, Kierkegaard's style of writing effects a singular way of doing

---

[34] 'There is/ it gives' attempts to give an English rendering of the ambiguity of the German 'es gibt', literally meaning 'it gives' but used in the sense of 'there is'. This is the theme of the other major essay in Vol. 14 of the *Gesamtausgabe*, 'Zeit und Sein' (Time and Being).

[35] In face of the dissatisfaction with Heidegger's 'non-Kierkegardian' paper, Beaufret concludes the second roundtable discussion by reminding his colleagues that he was only the translator and reader and that the UNESCO organizers had agreed beforehand that 'a paper by Heidegger on his own thought was the best homage that he could render to Kierkegaard' (Maheu, 1966: 313).

philosophy that exists in tension with more formal approaches – "in the margins of philosophy" as deconstructionists might have said. And, as Heidegger anticipates with regard to his own proposals, Kierkegaard too has predictably been charged with "mysticism" and "ruinous irrationalism"!

I have one further suggestion to add to Beaufret's remarks. We earlier noted Heidegger's praise for Kierkegaard's methodological "rigor" and analyzed this in terms of what Heidegger saw as Kierkegaard's persistence in focusing on the "how" in such a way as to penetrate into the pre-structuring of experience by a pre-reflective existential comportment. This is not "method" in the sense of applying a set of standard procedures to a given subject-matter but a matter of attentiveness to what a given view of reality omits, overlooks, or discards as irrelevant, that is, what is not included in the whole that presents itself as if it were the whole picture: it is the readiness to go on questioning beyond the point at which the consensus declares that there is nothing more to see. If this – or something like this – is in play in Heidegger's paper, then we can see how, despite all the differences with which we are now familiar, the "impulse" that Heidegger received from Kierkegaard may have continued to be effective in his thinking long beyond the time when the problematic of *Being and Time* had mutated into a sustained meditation on the mystery of the "There is/ it gives." On this point, it is probably far from coincidental that it is just this topic that has provided the occasion for the renewal of Christian apologetics on the ground of phenomenology (see, e.g., Marion, 2002).

5.5 Writing and Philosophy

We have several times now noted Heidegger's contempt for the Kierkegaard commentary of his day. At the same time, although we cannot accuse him of a simplistic or unnuanced interpretation of Kierkegaard's thought, and although he places Kierkegaard outside philosophy, it is (perhaps inevitably) from within the perspective of philosophy that he himself reads and evaluates his thought. But is this line of approach itself misleading as regards the real import of Kierkegaardian thought? It is perfectly possible to affirm Heidegger's view that Kierkegaard was not a philosopher and to agree that his primary interest was the sphere of Christian existence but it is also open to question whether Kierkegaard's approach to Christian existence was in any conventional sense *theological*, if we understand that term as applying to a certain academic discipline or "ontic science."

Kierkegaard was, of course, theologically educated and could use the language of theology with great facility. At the same time, he did not use them in the same way as theologians of a more academic character use them. It is precisely because the subjective thinker is focused on the "how" rather than the "what" that Kierkegaard's pseudonym Johannes Climacus emphasizes the thinker's "style" (Kierkegaard, 1992: 349–60) and for Kierkegaard this involved irony, humor, narrative, affective pathos, and moral appeal as much as conceptual analysis or phenomenological interpretation. As Kierkegaard said, writing in the voice of Johannes Climacus and commenting on a review of that pseudonym's *Philosophical Fragments*, "[The reviewer's] report is accurate and on the whole dialectically reliable, but now comes the hitch: although the report is accurate, anyone who reads only that will receive an utterly wrong impression of the book." This is because it misses "the contrast of form, the teasing resistance of the imaginary construction to the content, the inventive audacity (which even invents Christianity), the only attempt made to go further (i.e., further than the so-called speculative constructing), the indefatigable activity of irony, the parody of speculation in the entire plan, the satire in making efforts as if something *ganz Auszerordentliches und zwar Neues* were to come of them, whereas what always emerges is old-fashioned orthodoxy in its rightful severity – of all of this the reader finds no hint in the report" (Kierkegaard, 1992: 275).

It is in Kierkegaard's *style*, I suggest, that we see the most original aspect of his contribution to modern thought. This is not just a matter of the literary aspects of his work and has only in part to do with his use of pseudonyms and what he called indirect communication. Even within his directly (i.e., non-pseudonymous) religious writings he deploys a range of writerly tactics to disrupt and redirect his readers' relation to what they are reading. To take just one example, the way in which he writes about time doesn't just put a certain concept of time into play but challenges his readers' own time-experience. Perhaps the most obvious case of this relates to the very different styles of the two parts, or *Either/Or*. The first part (representing the aesthetic point of view) typically veers towards the aphoristic, replicating the disjointedness consequent upon the failure of the aesthete to commit to any unifying life-project. The second part (representing the ethical point of view) is presented in two long (many readers would say over-long) letters that are repetitive to the point of turgidity but thereby require the reader to engage with the slowness of our lived experience of time. But this is only a beginning. In other works, Kierkegaard plays with the sequencing and dating of the events they narrate, switches genres midstream, changes the direction and pace of his argument from the long-winded to the aphoristic (and back again), and uses images, parables, and stories that demand thoughtful interpretation and sometimes defy interpretation altogether (how can one interpret the absurd?). Here too, we might mention the insistent questions addressed to the reader: "Is it not so . . . ?" "Would you not ... ?" "Have you too not experienced ... ?," questions that alert us to the requirement to respond in our own way and according to our own evaluation of what is being said. We are not neutral observers of what is unfolding on the page before us but are again and again called out and addressed directly as "You."

Of course, it could be said that readers of Hegel or Heidegger are also challenged to stop, think, and ask themselves whether they really agree with what is being said. However – and, despite all the differences in their manner of arguing, this is as true of Heidegger as of Hegel – the philosophers' arguments are presented on the assumption that following the argument will lead the reader to accept its conclusions. To refuse the conclusion is to have failed to understand the sequence of steps, whether these are the movements of dialectical logic, the matter of phenomenological description, or the force of deep philology. No such necessity holds in our relation to the Kierkegaardian text and the possibility of disagreeing and even being scandalized by what is being said is written into the text itself. The obligation to submit to the arguments that are being presented is, as it were, suspended and we are invited to free ourselves from the text. This is not only the case with regard to the use of pseudonyms but is emphasized in many of the prefaces to the upbuilding discourses that speak of the reader as completing the task of the "speaker." As Kierkegaard says on one occasion, the reader "breaks the spell on the letters, with his voice summons forth what the mute letters have on their lips, as it were, but are unable to express without great effort, stammering and stuttering." (Kierkegaard, 1990: 53). In this way, Kierkegaard envisages an interpretative freedom in the relationship between himself, qua author and his readers, although (of course) this freedom is not and cannot be absolute. Kierkegaard himself wrote that only God is able to create in such a way that His creatures are completely free in relation to Him (Kierkegaard, 1997a: 127–28). A human text, by way of contrast, will always have some trace of its author and can only ever approximate the entire liberative action that a Word of God might accomplish. Neither the author nor the reader is able to follow through to a completely fulfilled freedom. As long as they are living in time, both are still underway, and both are and will remain learners. The pedagogy that Kierkegaard exercises is neither that of the apostle, nor the ordained priest, nor the professor, but is entirely without authority, the kind of instruction that can be offered by a friend and fellow learner – a pedagogy that Kierkegaard himself frequently called Socratic.[36]

I am not claiming that Heidegger was devoid of Socratic moments nor that he was entirely inattentive to Kierkegaard's style, his writerly "how," but it cannot

---

[36] It is relevant to add that the majority of Heidegger's works in the *Gesamtausgabe* were given as or in preparation for lectures and seminars, i.e., oral delivery, a difference that would not have been lost on Kierkegaard, who was highly conscious of the writerly character of his work.

be said that he paid explicit attention to this.[37] Heidegger undertook experi-
ments of his own regarding "poetic thinking" and his studies of Hölderlin and
other poets make up an essential part of his later thought. In this regard, it is all
the more interesting that he does not really advert to Kierkegaard's style in any
of his comments, except perhaps when he says that it is impossible to write
a book about Kierkegaard. He does not criticize Jaspers' interpretation of
Kierkegaard for the fact that it makes Kierkegaard into a philosopher but rather
that he secularizes Kierkegaard's idea of transcendence. At the same time, he
emphasizes that his own reading is framed by the overriding focus on being and
not the individual's concern for his own authentic being (GA96: 215–6). There
are profound resonances between Heidegger's and Kierkegaard's bodies of
work but, in the end, there are – as Heidegger himself recognized – no less
fundamental differences that are the result not only of Kierkegaard's specifically Christian orientation but also of their very different conceptions of the task
of philosophy and philosophical writing.

---

[37] He did, however, make what I find a useful comment on the pseudonyms, distinguishing between
the kind of "false name" assumed by someone who wishes to enhance their social status by
adopting an aristocratic name (I once knew someone who introduced himself as a Marquis,
though his title was not to be found in any recognized list of peerages) and a pseudonym, such as
Kierkegaard's, that, in Heidegger's words, "covers up, but in such a way that it indicates
simultaneously the recondite, concealed essence of the author and his literary task" (GA54:
53/36).

Texts and Methods of Citation

Page references to Heidegger's works will normally be given in brackets in the text, preceded by the Gesamtausgabe (GA) volume number and, where available, the relevant English translation.

SZ *Sein und Zeit*. Tübingen: Niemeyer, 1967. English translation: *Being and Time*. Translated by John Macquarrie and Edward Robinson. Oxford: Blackwell, 1962.

GA8 *Was Heisst Denken? Gesamtausgabe*, Volume 8. Edited by Paola-Ludovika Coriando. Frankfurt am Main: Klostermann, 2002. English translation: *What is Called Thinking?* Translated by J. Glenn Gray. New York: Harper and Row, 1968.

GA9 *Wegmarken. Gesamtausgabe*, Volume 9. Edited by Friedrich-Wilhelm von

Herrmann. Frankfurt am Main: Klostermann, 1976. English translation: *Pathmarks*. Edited by William McNeill. Cambridge: Cambridge University Press, 1998.

GA11 *Identität und Differenz*. Gesamtausgabe, Volume 11. Edited by Friedrich-Wilhelm

von Herrmann. Frankfurt am Main: Klostermann, 2006. English translation: *Identity and Difference*. Translated by Joan Stambaugh. New York: Harper and Row, 1969.

GA14 *Zur Sache des Denkens*. Gesamtausgabe, Volume 14. Edited by Friedrich-Wilhelm von Herrmann. Frankfurt am Main: Klostermann, 2007. English translation in David Farrell Krell, ed. *Martin Heidegger: Basic Writings*. London: Routledge, 1978, 369–92.

GA28 *Der deutsche Idealismus (Fichte, Schelling, Hegel) und die philosophische Problemlage der Gegenwart*. Edited by Claudius Strube. Frankfurt am Main: Klostermann, 1983.

GA29/30 *Die Grundbegriffe der Meataphysik. Welt – Endlichkeit – Einsamkeit. Gesamtausgabe*, Volume 29/30. Edited by Friedrich-Wilhelm von Hermann. Frankfurt am Main: Klostermann, 1983. English translation: *The Fundamental Concepts of Metaphysics: World, Finitude, Solitude*. Translated by William McNeill and Nicholas Walker. Bloomington, IN: Indiana University Press, 1995.

GA36/37   *Sein und Wahrheit. Gesamtausgabe*, Volume 36/37. Edited by Hartmut Tietjen. Frankfurt am Main: Klostermann, 2001.

GA42   *Schelling: Vom Wesen der menschlichen Freiheit (1809). Gesamtausgabe*, Volume 42. Edited by Ingrid Schüssler. Frankfurt am Main: Klostermann, 1988.

GA49   *Die Metaphysik des deutschen Idealismus (Schelling). Gesamtausgabe*, Volume 49. Edited by Günther Seubold. Frankfurt am Main: Klostermann, 2006.

GA55   *Parmenides. Gesamtausgabe*, Volume 49. Edited by Manfred S. Frings. Frankfurt am Main: Klostermann, 1994. English translation: *Parmenides*. Translated by André Schuwer and Richard Rojcewicz. Bloomington: Indiana University Press, 1998.

GA60   *Phänomenologie des religiösen Lebens. Gesamtausgabe*, Volume 60. Edited by Matthias Jung, Thomas Regehly, and Claudius Strube. Frankfurt am Main: Klostermann, 1995.

GA 63   *Ontologie. Hermeneutik der Faktizität. Gesamtausgabe*, Volume 63. Edited by Käte Bröcker-Oltmanns. Frankfurt am Main: Klostermann, 1995.

GA86   *Seminare: Hegel – Schelling. Gesamtausgabe*, Volume 86. Edited by Peter Trawny. Frankfurt am Main: Klostermann, 2011.

GA96   *Überlegungen XII-XV* (Schwarze Hefte 1939–1941). *Gesamtausgabe*, Volume 96. Edited by Peter Trawny. Frankfurt am Main: Klostermann, 2014.

GA97   *Anmerkungen VI-IX (Schwarze Hefte 1948/49–1951). Gesamtausgabe*, Volume 97. Edited by Peter Trawny. Frankfurt am Main: Klostermann, 2018.

References

Barnett, Christopher B. (2019). *Kierkegaard and the Question Concerning Technology*, New York: Bloomsbury.

Bernasconi, Robert (2021). Releasement (Gelassenheit). In Mark A. Wrathall, ed., *The Cambridge Heidegger Lexicon*, Cambridge: Cambridge University Press, pp. 629–31.

Caputo, John D. (1986). *The Mystical Element in Heidegger's Thought*, New York: Fordham University Press.

Dahlstrom, Daniel (2010). Freedom through Despair: Kierkegaard's Phenomenological Analysis. In Jeffrey Hanson, ed., *Kierkegaard as Phenomenologist: An Experiment*, Evanston, IL: Northwestern University Press, pp. 57–78.

Dreyfus, Hubert L. (2009). *On the Internet*, London: Routledge.

Grøn, Arne (2023). *Thinking with Kierkegaard: Existential Philosophy, Phenomenology and Ethics.* Kierkegaard Studies Monograph Series, No. 44. Berlin: Walter de Gruyter.

Guérin, Benjamin (2011). Chestov – Kierkegaard: Faux ami, étranger fraternité. In Ramona Fotiade and Françoise Schwab, eds., *Léon Chestov – Vladimir Jankélévitch: Du tragique à l'ineffable*, Saarbrücken: Éditions universitaires européennes.

Guignon, Charles (2011). Heidegger and Kierkegaard on Death: The Existentiell and the Existential. In Patrick Stokes and Adam Buben, eds., *Kierkegaard and Death*, Bloomington, IN: Indiana University Press, 184–203.

Han-Pile, Beatrice (2013). Freedom and the "Choice to Choose Oneself." In Mark A. Wrathall, ed., *The Cambridge Companion to Being and Time*, Cambridge: Cambridge University Press, pp. 291–319.

Heidegger, Martin (1972). *Frühe Schriften*, Frankfurt am Main: Klostermann.

Heidegger, Martin (1978). *Basuc Writings*. Edited and translated by D. F. Krell. London: Routledge & Kegan Paul.

Hirsch, Emanuel (1933). *Kierkegaard-Studien* I. Gütersloh: Bertelsmann.

Kangas, David (2018). *Errant Affirmations: On the Philosophical Meaning of Kierkegaard's Religious Discourses*, London: Bloomsbury.

Kangas, David (2007). *Kierkegaard's Instant: On Beginnings*, Bloomington, IN: Indiana University Press.

Khawaja, Noreen (2015). Heidegger's Kierkegaard: Philosophy and Religion in the Tracks of a Failed Interpretation. *The Journal of Religion*, Vol. 95, No. 3, 295–317.

64   *References*

Khawaja, Noreen (2016). *The Religion of Existence: Asceticism in Philosophy from Kierkegaard to Sartre*, Chicago, IL: Chicago University Press.

Kierkegaard, Søren (1997a). *Christian Discourses: The Crisis and a Crisis in the Life of an Actress*, trans. H. V. and E. H. Hong, Princeton: Princeton University Press.

Kierkegaard, Søren (1980a). *The Concept of Anxiety*, trans. R. Thomte, Princeton: Princeton University Press.

Kierkegaard, Søren (1992). *Concluding Unscientific Postscript*, trans. H. V. and E. H. Hong, Princeton: Princeton University Press.

Kierkegaard, Søren (1990). *Eighteen Upbuilding Discourses*, trans. H. V. and E. H. Hong, Princeton: Princeton University Press.

Kierkegaard, Søren (1987). *Either/Or*, trans. H. V. and E. H. Hong, Princeton: Princeton University Press.

Kierkegaard, Søren (1983). *Fear and Trembling/Repetition*, trans. H. V. and E. H. Hong, Princeton: Princeton University Press.

Kierkegaard, Søren (1998a). *The Moment and Late Writings*, trans. H. V. and E. H. Hong, Princeton: Princeton University Press.

Kierkegaard, Søren (1998b). *The Point of View*, trans. H. V. and E. H. Hong, Princeton: Princeton University Press.

Kierkegaard, Søren (1980b). *The Sickness unto Death*, trans. H. V. and E. H. Hong, Princeton: Princeton University Press.

Kierkegaard, Søren (1993a). *Three Discourses on Imagined Occasions*, trans. H. V. and E. H. Hong, Princeton: Princeton University Press.

Kierkegaard, Søren (1978). *Two Ages*, trans. H. V. and E. H. Hong, Princeton: Princeton University Press.

Kierkegaard, Søren (1993b). *Upbuilding Discourses in Various Spirits*, trans. H. V. and E. H. Hong, Princeton: Princeton University Press.

Kierkegaard, Søren (1997b). *Without Authority*, trans. H. V. and E. H. Hong, Princeton: Princeton University Press.

Kierkegaard, Søren (1995). *Works of Love*, trans. H. V. and E. H. Hong, Princeton: Princeton University Press.

Kirkpatrick, Matthew (2011). *Attacks on Christendom in a World Come of Age: Kierkegaard, Bonhoeffer, and the Question of "Religionless Christianity,"* Eugene, OR: Pickwick.

Kisiel, Theodore and Sheehan, Thomas (2007). *Becoming Heidegger: On the Trail of His Early Occasional Writings, 1910–1927*, Bloomington, IN: Northwestern University Press.

Löwith, Karl (1995). *Heidegger and European Nihilism*, trans. Gary Steiner, New York: Columbia University Press.

Maheu, René, ed. (1966). *Kierkegaard Vivant*, Paris: Gallimard.

Malik, Habib (1997). *Receiving Søren Kierkegaard: The Early Impact and Transmission of His Thought*, Washington, DC: Catholic Universities of America Press.

Mann, Thomas (1949). *Doctor Faustus*, trans. H. T. Lowe-Porter, London: Secker and Warburg.

Marcel, Gabriel (1950). *The Mystery of Being. I. Reflection & Mystery*, London: The Harvill Press.

Marion, Jean-Luc (2002). *Being Given: Toward a Phenomenology of Givenness*, trans. Jeffrey L. Kosky, Stanford: Stanford University Press.

Pattison, George (2013a). *Heidegger on Death: A Critical Theological Essay*, Farnham: Ashgate.

Pattison, George (2006). Heidegger's Hölderlin and Kierkegaard's Christ. In Stephen Mulhall, ed., *Martin Heidegger*, Farnham: Ashgate, pp. 391–404.

Pattison, George (2013b). *Kierkegaard and the Quest for Unambiguous Life: Between Romanticism and Modernism Selected Essay*, Oxford: Oxford University Press.

Pattison, George (2019). *A Rhetorics of the Word: A Philosophy of Christian Life Part 2*, Oxford: Oxford University Press.

Ryan, Bartholomew (2014). *Kierkegaard's Indirect Politics: Interludes with Lukács, Schmitt, Benjamin and Adorno*. Amsterdam: Rodolpi.

Schleiermacher, Friedrich Daniel Ernst (1989). *The Christian Faith*, trans. H. R. Mackintosh and J. Stewart, Edinburgh: T & T Clark.

Schmitt, Carl (2004). *Politische Theologie. Vier Kapitel zur Lehre von der Souveranität*, Berlin, Duncker & Humboldt.

Schulz, Heiko (2009). Germany and Austria: A Modest Head Start: The German Reception of Kierkegaard. In Jon Stewart, ed., *Kierkegaard's International Reception: Northern and Western Europe: Kierkegaard Research: Sources, Reception and Resources*, Vol. 8, Tome I, Farnham: Ashgate, pp. 307–419.

Schürmann, Reiner (2001). *Wandering Joy: Meister Eckhart's Mystical Theology*, Great Barrington, MA: Lindisfarne Books.

Theunissen, Michael (2006). The Upbuilding in the Thought of Death: Traditional Elements, Innovative Ideas, and Unexhausted Possibilities in Kierkegaard's "At a Graveside," trans. George Pattison. In Robert L. Perkins, ed., *International Kierkegaard Commentary, Volume 10: Three Discourses on Imagined Occasions*. Macon, GA: Mercer University Press, pp. 321–58.

Thonhauser, Gerhard (2016). *Ein Rätselhaftes Zeichen: Zum Verhältnis von Martin Heidegger und Søren Kierkegaard*. Kierkegaard Studies Monograph Series, No. 33, Berlin: Walter de Gruyter.

Tillich, Paul (1956). *The Religious Situation*, trans. H. Richard Niebuhr, New York: Meridian Books.

Wolfe, Judith (2014). *Heidegger and Theology*, London: Bloomsbury T&T Clark.

Wyschogrod, Michael (1954). *Kierkegaard and Heidegger: The Ontology of Existence*, New York: The Humanities Press.

Acknowledgements

I am grateful to Filippo Casati and Daniel Dahlstrom for the opportunity to write this little book. The Kierkegaard-Heidegger connection is one that has preoccupied me over many years and this has been a great opportunity to get some order into widely dispersed thoughts and to come back to the relevant texts – I do not, however, claim fully to have resolved key questions and it remains an open question as to whether some are, in fact, resolvable. I have been greatly helped by Gerhard Thonhauser's 2016 study *Ein Rätselhaftes Zeichen* (*A Riddlesome Sign*), a meticulous work of scholarship on the Kierkegaard–Heidegger relationship that provides a clear and exhaustive account of Heidegger's knowledge of Kierkegaard and tracks references throughout his works. Naturally, Thonhauser's work doesn't answer all questions and there remains considerable scope for wide divergences of opinion, depending not least on the interpreter's overall view as to the respective worth and interest of the two authors. Each can be and has been put to service in very different philosophical, cultural, and spiritual undertakings, allowing for multiple interpretative possibilities – but Thonhauser's work means that we now have solid ground under our feet.

The Philosophy of Martin Heidegger

About the Editors

Filippo Casati

Lehigh University

Filippo Casati is an Assistant Professor at Lehigh University. He has published an array of articles in such venues as The British Journal for the History of Philosophy, Synthese, Logic et Analyse, Philosophia, Philosophy Compass and The European Journal of Philosophy. He is the author of Heidegger and the Contradiction of Being (Routledge) and, with Daniel O. Dahlstrom, he edited Heidegger on logic (Cambridge University Press).

Daniel O. Dahlstrom

Boston University

Daniel O. Dahlstrom, John R. Silber Professor of Philosophy at Boston University, has edited twenty volumes, translated Mendelssohn, Schiller, Hegel, Husserl, Heidegger, and Landmann-Kalischer, and authored Heidegger's Concept of Truth (2001), The Heidegger Dictionary (2013; second extensively expanded edition, 2023), Identity, Authenticity, and Humility (2017) and over 185 essays, principally on 18th-20th century German philosophy. With Filippo Casati, he edited Heidegger on Logic (Cambridge University Press).

About the Series

A continual source of inspiration and controversy, the work of Martin Heidegger challenges thinkers across traditions and has opened up previously unexplored dimensions of Western thinking. The Elements in this series critically examine the continuing impact and promise of a thinker who transformed early twentieth-century phenomenology, spawned existentialism, gave new life to hermeneutics, celebrated the truthfulness of art and poetry, uncovered the hidden meaning of language and being, warned of "forgetting" being, and exposed the ominously deep roots of the essence of modern technology in Western metaphysics. Concise and structured overviews of Heidegger's philosophy offer original and clarifying approaches to the major themes of Heidegger's work, with fresh and provocative perspectives on its significance for contemporary thinking and existence.

Cambridge Elements ☰

The Philosophy of Martin Heidegger

Elements in the Series

A full series listing is available at: www.cambridge.org/EPMH

Printed in the United States
by Baker & Taylor Publisher Services